Elite • 159

French Napoleonic Infantry Tactics 1792–1815

Paddy Griffith • Illustrated by Peter Dennis

Consultant editor Martin Windrow

OSPREY PUBLISHING
Bloomsbury Publishing Plc

Kemp House, Chawley Park, Oxford OX2 9PH, UK
29 Earlsfort Terrace, Dublin 2, Ireland
1385 Broadway, 5th Floor, New York, NY 10018, USA
Email: info@ospreypublishing.com
www.ospreypublishing.com

OSPREY is a trademark of Osprey Publishing Ltd

First published in Great Britain in 2007
Transferred to digital print in 2014

© Osprey Publishing Ltd, 2007

A catalogue record for this book is available from the British Library

Print ISBN: 978 1 84603 278 3
ePDF: 978 1 78200 249 9
ePub: 978 1 78200 223 9

Editorial by Martin Windrow
Page layouts by Ken Vail Graphic Design, Cambridge, UK
Index by Glyn Sutcliffe
Originated by PPS Grasmere, Leeds, UK
Typeset in Helvetica Neue and ITC New Baskerville
Printed and bound in India by Replika Press Private Ltd.

MIX
Paper from responsible sources
FSC® C016779

24 25 26 27 28   15 14 13 12 11 10

The Woodland Trust
Osprey Publishing supports the Woodland Trust, the UK's leading woodland conservation charity.

Dedication
For Jean Lochet, whose *Empires, Eagles and Lions* has left a major intellectual legacy in this field. He tells me that he is a distant relative of the General Lochet who fought at Austerlitz and Auerstadt, and who was killed at Eylau.

Acknowledgements
I am particularly grateful to Philip Haythornthwaite, of North Lancashire, not only for supplying illustrations but also for his great help and expertise over many years. Thanks also to Peter Harrington of the Anne S.K.Brown Library for supplying illustrations.

For my early studies in this field I owe a great debt to Norman Gibbs, Piers Mackesy and the staff of the Bodleian, Codrington and RMA Sandhurst libraries. Then came Jean Lochet with his wonderful *EEL*, in all its various formats and with all its fascinating contributors. Not least, my gratitude goes to Ned Zuparko, who has recently introduced me to *The Napoleon Series at http://www.napoleon-series.org.*

I am also grateful to all who have accompanied me on battlefield tours to the French battlefields of 1792-1815 – most notably to my son Robert, who, at the age of 3, had an extreme and surprising reaction to visiting the field of Sorauren. I am also, of course and as always, a great admirer of René Mouriaux, one of whose lesser services on my behalf was that he took me to visit the grave of Chatrian.

Artist's note
Readers may care to note that the original paintings from which the colour plates in this book were prepared are available for private sale. All reproduction copyright whatsoever is retained by the Publishers. All enquiries should be addressed to:

Peter Dennis, Fieldhead, The Park, Mansfield, Notts NG18 2AT, UK

Or email: magie.h@ntlworld.com

The Publishers regret that they can enter into no correspondence upon this matter.

www.ospreypublishing.com
To find out more about our authors and books visit our website. Here you will find extracts, author interviews, details of forthcoming events and the option to sign-up for our newsletter.

GLOSSARY OF ENGLISH TERMS
French terms are explained on page 4 or where they first appear in the text

deploy – to change formation, in one way or another, from column to line.
Division – a major formation consisting of several brigades or regiments, within an Army Corps. It is conventional to give this a capital 'D' in this context.
division – a manoeuvre unit of two platoons operating in line abreast. Before 1808 there were four divisions per French battalion, but after 1808 just three. It is conventional to use the lower case 'd' in this context.
file – a line of troops standing one behind the other, from front to rear.
interval – either the distance from front to rear between ranks, sub-units and units; or the sideways distance between one unit or sub-unit and the next.

line – In 'minor tactics' terms this refers to a battalion in deployed formation three deep, as opposed to some more concentrated and deeper column. In 'grand tactics' terms its meaning is utterly different: it refers to the reserves held behind the front line. The 'second line' was usually held in a line of battalion columns, and the 'third line', if there was one, was supposed to be in a 'brigade mass'.

ploy – to change formation, in one way or another, from line to column.

rank – a single line of troops standing side by side. Normally there would be three ranks, one behind the other, in each platoon.

FRENCH NAPOLEONIC INFANTRY TACTICS 1792-1815

THE LEGACY OF THE SEVEN YEARS' WAR

THIS is a book about the way French infantry actually fought, from the start of the Revolution all the way through to Waterloo; and about the way its leaders thought it ought to fight – which was not always the same thing at all. There was always a tension between practice and theory, just as there was between tactics that depended on shock action and those that depended on firepower. There were further wide variations in approach from one individual commander to another, and from one type of battle to another. The tactics that could be executed by experienced and well-trained troops were much more complicated than those that were within the grasp of freshly raised or second-line troops.

During the period 1792–1815 the French fielded many different armies in many different theatres, and their quality was far from uniform.

The veteran Grande Armée that marched out of the Boulogne camp in the autumn of 1805 was one of the best exercised and most manoeuvrable forces ever seen in the whole of military history. By contrast, most members of the two Young Guard Divisions that were fed into the battle at Craonne on 7 March 1814 (known as 'Marie Louises', after Bonaparte's virginal second wife) had been pressed into the army only a month earlier.

During the 1790s the French armies were often relatively inexperienced, and even ramshackle in terms of their logistics and supply arrangements; yet at least they were usually led by well-trained commanders. Admittedly, a few of the generals were incompetent political appointments, while an even smaller minority were brilliant natural leaders who rose rapidly through the ranks to find the proverbial 'marshal's baton in their knapsacks'.[1] However, between these two extremes the vast majority of French generals were good soldiers and noblemen (more or less), who had received a long induction into the classic military culture and tactics of the Ancien Régime. They had attended royal schools and had spent time in the headquarters of the king's armies.

---

[1] The original French phrase should be translated literally as 'cartridge box', but in English this version has become traditional.

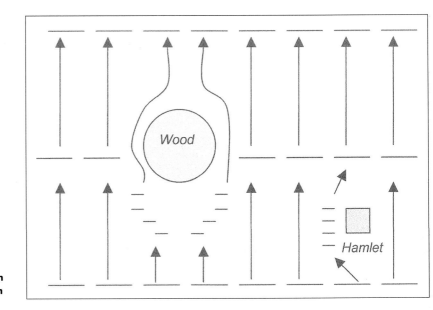

The legacy of the Seven Years, War: an advance by a Division of eight battalions in a single line, with a frontage of about 1,500 yards. Each battalion is fully deployed in a three-deep line, attempting to keep alignment with its neighbours on either side. This type of manoeuvre was the basis of much 18th-century thinking about tactics, and was difficult enough on a flat, empty field. In practice, most real battlefields were obstructed by woods, buildings, enclosures, water obstacles and slopes, which made smooth evolutions of the line impossibly demanding. In order to keep moving, a battalion in line would have to break down temporarily into some form of column – by divisions, platoons, or even smaller groups – and then re-form into line after passing the obstacle. Each such miniature manoeuvre significantly disrupted the advance as a whole, and during the period after 1791 it was often found easier to move all battalions in column and deploy into line only at the last moment.

Bonaparte himself was no exception, although his extreme youth when he first rose to prominence has perhaps obscured this fact (he was 24 years old at the siege of Toulon in 1793).

It is important to remember that the military thinking of the Ancien Régime had been very significantly moulded by French experiences during the Seven Years' War (1756–63). Many fruitful debates had been generated then which had already – long before the First Empire – placed the French well in the forefront of the most modern 'art of war' as it was internationally understood. Marc-René Montalembert had designed an innovative system of casemated fortification, and Jean Baptiste Vaquette de Gribeauval had designed and built some of the best mobile artillery in the world. At the level of strategy, staffwork and operations, Pierre Bourcet had written a textbook on warfare in the Alps that would become very much a 'set text' for the young Bonaparte.

At the level of tactics, an enormously important lesson from the Seven Years' War – particularly the French-Indian War in America – and from

The organization of units and formations

company or platoon – Both terms refer to the basic unit of around 100 infantry, intended to be commanded by a captain. Theoretically the company was an administrative unit while the platoon was a tactical unit, although the two words are often treated as interchangeable.

division – Two companies or platoons in line, manoeuvring together as a single unit.

battalion – A tactical unit commanded by a major or lieutenant-colonel. In theory each battalion should have 8 platoons (or 9, if we include the grenadier platoon that was often detached), each of 114 men, making a total of 912 (or 1,026). In early 1808 this was changed to 6 platoons each of 140 men, including one of grenadiers and one of voltigeurs, making a total of 840. In practice, on campaign, the combat strength of a battalion often fell to 500 or fewer, and sometimes even as low as 200 men.

regiment – A parent administrative unit, commanded by a colonel, which had a depot in France from which one or more battalions would be sent out to theatres of war. Sometimes two, three or even as many as six battalions of a regiment would fight together: at other times they might each be detached separately to different theatres. During much of the 1790s an attempt was made to put three battalions into the field together as what was in effect a 'regiment', but which at that time was termed a demi-brigade ('half-brigade').

brigade – A tactical unit of two or more battalions, under a brigade general. Presumably at one time there had been an idea that two demi-brigades should make a whole brigade, but in practice there was absolutely no uniformity.

Division – A formation of two or more brigades, often with artillery or even cavalry attached, under a division general (see also Glossary, p.2).

Corps – A formation of two or more Divisions, with all arms attached, under a lieutenant-general or (from 1804) a marshal.

the American Revolutionary War, had been the great value of skirmishers. In difficult terrain where formal close-order drill was impossible, well-trained snipers or marksmen *(tirailleurs)*, rangers or 'hunters' *(chasseurs)*, scouts *(éclaireurs)*, or simply light infantry *(infanterie légère)* often proved invaluable. During the 1790s and 1800s a number of other supposedly specialized types would be added, most famously the 'jumpers' *(voltigeurs)*, who were supposed to enter battle riding pillion behind a cavalryman and then leap off to open a galling musketry fire upon the enemy.

Such fantasies were laughably impractical, and in the fiery crucible of real campaigning all these intended varieties and distinctions immediately evaporated. The troops designated for light infantry work should more realistically be classified, firstly, according to whether they fought in line (i.e. in close order) or as skirmishers (i.e. in open order); and then, if they did in fact fight as skirmishers, they should be graded on how carefully they had been trained for that specialized role. In the period 1792–1815 one suspects that many of the supposedly 'light' troops were actually used as 'heavy' infantry; and many of those who really were used in the light role had received absolutely no training for it. This was perhaps unsurprising, in view of the absence of any official army-wide manual on how skirmishing should be conducted.

Line and column – 'the great arguments'

However, the most heated tactical debates to be sparked by the Seven Years' War were centred on how the 'heavy' infantry should fight, and these would tellingly become known as *'les grandes querelles'*. During the early part of the 18th century, the conventional wisdom had been that infantry should conduct both its approach march and then its combat action in lines three deep. This arrangement had the advantage of maximizing the continuous frontage that could be occupied on the battlefield, since, with a density of three men per 22 inches – each touching elbows with his neighbours – an army of 60,000 men could occupy a frontage of no less than 13km, or a little over 8 miles. Even allowing for a second or reserve line, the frontage would be 6.5km or almost 4.5 miles – which is still a major piece of real estate. A second, and possibly even more important advantage of the line formation was that, at least in theory, every soldier would be able to fire his musket or point his bayonet in a meaningful way.

In practice the third rank, and to some extent the second rank too, tended to find it somewhat difficult to fire or stab 'through' the front rank, and there were some reports of nasty injuries being inflicted on the latter. Nevertheless, it was normally deemed best to stick to three ranks rather than two (let alone one, although a few examples of both may be found in Napoleonic

A regular infantry drummer, c.1790–92, as portrayed by Jean-Frédéric Striedbeck, the first publisher of sheets of 'paper soldiers' in Strasbourg. The drummer is symbolically posted just beside his officer, who will issue the orders that the drummer will broadcast to the soldiers who have to execute them. In the 1791 drill manual, however, all the drums of a battalion would be collected in one group to the rear, close to the battalion commander, rather than being left in their individual platoons – each platoon captain would thus be a recipient of drum signals, rather an originator of them. (Philip Haythornthwaite Collection)

A platoon of Imperial Guardsmen firing at will in a three-deep line. In the *Règlement* the first volley fired by each platoon was supposed to be simultaneous by each file, immediately followed by the next file, and so on, rolling along the platoon line. After that, everyone was supposed to fire at will at their own speed. This could vary widely, since the 1791 manual specified about 25 separate movements for loading and firing a single shot. This picture is based closely on the *Règlement,* with the platoon officer in his regulation place on the right flank; the men in the foreground stand straight upright with their feet correctly placed at right-angles, and the men of the second rank pass back their muskets to be reloaded by the third rank – an image perhaps more faithful to the regulations than to actual practice. Note also the man firing from the second rank over the left shoulder of his comrade – biting open a cartridge – in the front rank. Another perhaps idealized detail is the careful aim taken by individual soldiers, in an age when men got little target practice, and the battle-lines were blinded by powder-smoke. (After Bellange; Philip Haythornthwaite Collection)

times), since the extra men in rear would provide moral support to the men in front, as well as physical file-fillers who could step forward to plug gaps in the event of heavy casualties. The 'solidity' of a three-deep line was deemed to be especially required when there was a serious threat from cavalry.

The line was thus the 'classic' or conventional formation for infantry, and it implied a battle based on firepower. Yet the disadvantage was that it was always difficult to keep a line in position unless a long time was spent in checking and re-checking its alignments. The task of maintaining every

One aspect of the 'column vs. line' debate was the effect of artillery fire against each. A relatively shallow formation would obviously expect to suffer fewer casualties from roundshot than a relatively deep formation. Both, if they had the same frontage, could expect similar casualties from roundshot fired in enfilade along the ranks from a flank. However, there was some room for debate over the effects of grape or canister, which tended to hit mainly the front rank. In such cases, as with enfilades, it was arguable that casualties would be fairly similar regardless of the formation.

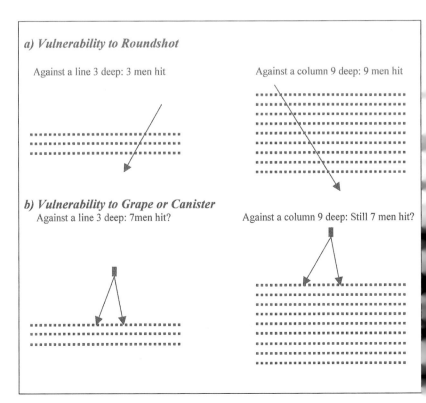

a) Vulnerability to Roundshot

Against a line 3 deep: 3 men hit

Against a column 9 deep: 9 men hit

b) Vulnerability to Grape or Canister

Against a line 3 deep: 7men hit?

Against a column 9 deep: Still 7 men hit?

man in place over a 6-mile frontage was daunting indeed, and trebly so if they were all expected to move forwards, backwards or sideways in step with one another. Such a line was a formation that might potentially develop the highest firepower; but it was also a staff officer's nightmare, and no one could ever claim that it offered high tactical mobility.

These advantages and disadvantages were dissected in great detail in the course of *les grandes querelles,* especially once an alternative approach – in the form of a 'column' attack – had been put forward by a number of writers such as Louis-Pierre de Puysegur, Jean-Charles de Folard, François-Jean de Ménil-Durand, and then Joly de Maizeroy. These writers suggested that the infantry should fight in columns, to exploit the supposed shock effect of a concentrated mass attack. Columns were much easier to manoeuvre than lines, particularly over broken ground; and there was also a widespread belief that they were good for maintaining the morale of shaky troops, who would gain confidence by the close proximity of so many of their comrades.

The opponents of columns, such as Count Hippolyte de Guibert and the Chevalier Tronçon du Coudray, were quick to reply that they were far more vulnerable to artillery fire. A cannonball could theoretically knock down only one file of three men in a line, whereas there would be many more men per file in a column; a deep column might well suffer a dozen men hit by each accurate round. This whole question of vulnerability to artillery was extensively debated, with the partisans of the column pointing out that lines were exceptionally vulnerable to enfilades and even, to some extent, to grape and canister. On the whole, however, the balance of opinion was that it was more dangerous to fight in columns than in lines when facing an opponent with powerful artillery.

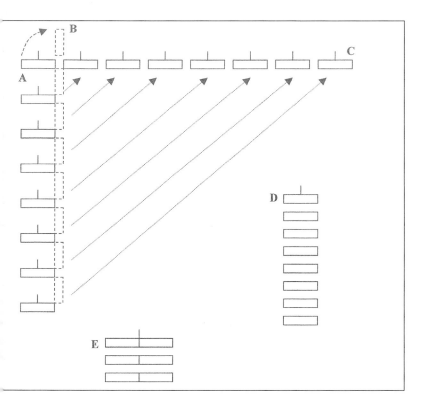

Two platoons of infantry – here, Polish troops of the later Empire – advancing with muskets shouldered in closed column of platoons (i.e., with only a small interval between one platoon and the one behind). The closed column gave greater solidity than the open column, but hampered easy deployments or other manoeuvres. (After Raffet; Philip Haythornthwaite Collection)

Various different types of column were suggested, ranging from a dense formation of a whole Division of 6,400 men with a frontage of 80 files and a depth of 80 ranks, to what would come to be called the 'column of attack' or column by divisions, consisting of a battalion of 912 men with a frontage of about 76 files and a depth of 12 ranks. During the wars of 1792–1815 not only would all the theoretical types of column be seen on actual battlefields, but many new types would be invented or improvised. Some of the 'monstrous' columns would contain many more troops than the notional 6,400 of a Division, whereas some battalion columns of attack might turn out to contain as few as 200 men, on a frontage of less than 33 and a depth of just 6 ranks. It could be argued that the latter layout was only slightly deeper than a regulation line, and it was certainly a very far cry from the heavy sledgehammer formations imagined by De Puysegur and his followers.

Despite all these complexities and ambiguities, the key point at issue in *les grandes querelles* seemed to be a clear choice between the column (*l'ordre profond*) and the line (*l'ordre mince*). At first the debate was confined to pamphlets and memoranda; but in 1778 it was extended to a series of trials, with 30,000 real soldiers manoeuvring against each other at the camp of Vaussieux, near Bayeux in Normandy, commanded by the free-thinking Marshal the Duke of Broglie. The results of the trials were ambiguous and bitterly contested, but at least the believers in the line were forced to admit that columns could often have an important role, as a formation for troops waiting in reserve or advancing rapidly into the front line. Once arrived in or near the front line, however, there remained a great deal of scepticism that columns were best for a firefight: they made big targets, and could develop only a small proportion of their own firepower.

GUIBERT AND THE 1791 *RÈGLEMENT*

Perhaps the most important figure in these debates was General Count Jacques-Antoine-Hippolyte de Guibert (1743–90), who had published his *Essai général de tactique* in 1770 (anonymously until the second edition, a couple of years later). Apart from being a controversial tactical writer, he was a noted ornament of literary society and was known for advanced social opinions. He had, for example, been an early prophet of the democratic mass conscription that would so soon become a central feature of the military system of France, and subsequently of all other continental powers. In 1787–89 he became the chief military adviser to the government, but at that time the reactionary royal establishment proved to be still unready for his opinions, and he was soon told to clear his desk. Guibert might have been re-employed more profitably in later republican times had he not died prematurely in May 1790, so his legacy remained theoretical rather than practical.

However, it was at least sufficient to enable an authoritative resolution to be imposed on *les grandes querelles* just before the outbreak of war in April 1792, when it would be badly needed. The document that eventually laid out the official tactics for the French infantry in the Revolutionary and Napoleonic wars, and then on into the 1830s, appeared on 1 August 1791. Entitled the *Règlement concernant l'exercice et les manoeuvres de l'infanterie* ('Manual for the training and manoeuvres of infantry'), or simply 'the *Règlement* of 1791', it owed more than a little to Guibert's guiding influence.

'The New Prussian Exercise', a British cartoon mocking the defeat of the Prussians at the battle of Valmy, 1792. For much of the 18th century the Prussians had taken the lead in infantry drill or 'exercise' and enjoyed an unequalled military reputation. The more distressing 'movements' shown in this example of typically scatological period humour are a reference to the Prussians suffering the after-effects of eating unripe apples during their retreat from France. (Anne S.K. Brown Library, Providence, RI)

The NEW PRUSSIAN EXERCISE or the Allied Armies Distressed in their REAR, with a hint at the Convenience of SANS Culottes
For Brunswick's Duke with Ninety Thousand Men
March'd into France and then ____ March'd out again,

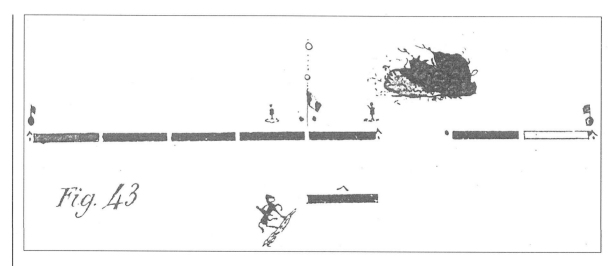

Fig. 43

A diagram from the 1831 revision of the 1791 *Règlement*. When a battalion advancing in line encountered an obstacle (as very frequently happened), one or more platoons had to double up behind a neighbouring platoon – a disruptive operation, especially under fire. Note the use not only of the flag in the centre of the battalion, but also of markers for alignment on the flanks. (Author's collection)

The *Règlement* remained essentially an 18th-century and conservative document, since it was based almost entirely upon the manoeuvres of the line. These could be extremely complex, and so they would require well-trained troops and exceptionally well trained drill-masters.

There were, nevertheless, a number of significant concessions to the column, and especially Guibert's own simplified system for passing a battalion quickly from the line to the column of attack, and back again.

There was practically no advice on how to use skirmishers; but there were some basic instructions on how to form squares against cavalry, which would be refined in later editions. The latter topic was a rare example in the *Règlement* of specific tactical manoeuvres being recommended against a specific tactical threat. More usually the details of particular manoeuvres were laid out, but with very little explanation of the circumstances in which it might be appropriate to use them.

It was taken as read, rather than spelled out, that a commander would always wish to fight with his troops in a line presenting a solid front of fire to the enemy. However, it was also accepted that he might need to use various complex combinations – including variants of the column – to bring them forward into the front line over broken ground, or from the roads on which they had originally approached the battlefield. The columns would ideally deploy into firing lines just before they came into musketry range of the enemy. Equally, if they were then to fall back they might need to shorten their frontage, by reverting to columns to allow a relieving second line to come forward and pass through the gaps. This manoeuvre was called 'the passage of lines', and it held a position of great importance in tactical theory, since it allowed a commander to replace tired and battered soldiers, who had used up their ammunition, with fresh and fully supplied men. Thus a battle could be continued in circumstances where otherwise it might be lost.

It is frustrating to the modern student that the intended relationship between the column and the line – i.e. column for manoeuvre, and line for combat – was never fully explained in the *Règlement,* so we cannot truly claim that it was the officially laid down system of the French Army as a whole. Nevertheless, there is so much circumstantial evidence that this is the way French generals thought about their battles that the conclusion is inescapable. It may not be easy to prove in the case of

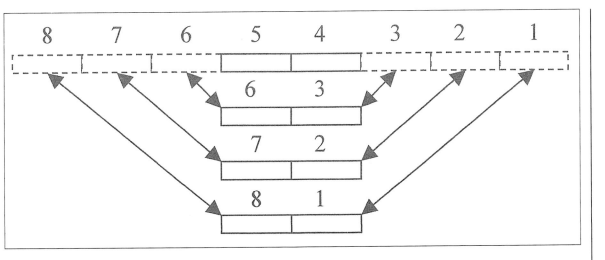

the first big battle of the Revolutionary wars – the defensive stand in the 'cannonade of Valmy' on 20 September 1792; but it was certainly clear in the second battle, which was fought on 6 November 1792 at Jemappes, near Mons (see Plate A).

On that occasion Gen Dumouriez was attacking, and he laid out his army precisely on the pattern of a line in front and a variety of columns in rear. His intentions were clear, and entirely in conformity with classic principles. He started with a heavy five-hour artillery bombardment, followed by an infantry attack all along the line at noon. At some points the troops were able to execute their 'classic' tactics; but at other points they could make no progress because they were so inexperienced, and lacked solid military cohesion. Some lines dissolved into skirmishing bands, and some columns dissolved into formless masses or 'blobs'. (Another dramatic example would come at Wattignies on 15 October 1793 – see Plate B).

At Jemappes the Austrians were outnumbered three to one (13,000 to 40,000), but inflicted over three times as many casualties as they suffered

COLUMN TO LINE
Among drill-masters, Guibert was famous for his 'column of attack', even though it is doubtful that he ever intended it as an assault formation. Its great virtue was that it allowed a compact column to deploy into line fairly quickly and easily, and for a line to ploy back again into column with equal ease. Purists were shocked that this column did not have the 1st and 2nd Platoons (by seniority) at the front, or even paired in the same division; but they were delighted that when it shook out into line the eight platoons were ordered correctly, from right to left in seniority.

Thumbnail chronology of Revolutionary and Napoleonic wars:

1792–97: The war of the First Coalition
France declares war on Austria and Prussia; beats off the Prussians at Valmy (1792), invades Belgium and the Rhineland. Spain and Britain join in (1793) but make little progress. 1793 sees crisis for the French Revolutionary régime on all fronts, including the Vendée, Lyon and Toulon; the crisis is overcome by the rule of 'Terror'. Bonaparte's Italian campaign (1796–97) brings peace.

1798–1802: The Second Coalition
Bonaparte's doomed Egyptian expedition (1798–1801); Austria and Russia attack in Italy and Switzerland (1799). Bonaparte becomes military dictator and retakes Italy at Marengo; Moreau is victorious in Germany (1800).

1804: The Boulogne Camp
Start of the Empire and revival of the Marshalate.

1805: The Third Coalition
Lightning march by the French Grande Armée from Boulogne to victory at Austerlitz over Russia and Austria.

1806–07: The Fourth Coalition
The Prussians are defeated at Jena (1806), and the Russians fought to a standstill in Poland (1807).

1808–14: The Peninsular War
French attempt to set up puppet régimes in Spain and Portugal is met by strong local resistance, with some British assistance. Attritional deadlock until the French are driven back over the Pyrenees in 1813.

1809: The Fifth Coalition
Austrian revolt is defeated at Wagram.

1812–14: The Sixth Coalition
Bonaparte invades Russia, to lose almost his entire Grande Armée there (1812). He improvises new armies as his German allies turn against him (Saxony campaign, 1813); Wellington's victory at Vitoria that year finally breaks the French grip on the Peninsula. The whole of Europe unites to drive Bonaparte back into France. He is finally defeated in the Champagne campaign (1814) and forced to abdicate, just before Wellington's final victory at Toulouse.

1815: The Hundred Days (or Seventh Coalition)
Bonaparte escapes from Elba and reclaims his throne, causing the whole of Europe to unite against him; he is totally defeated at Waterloo.

An unsigned lithograph illustrates a platoon line firing at will; it shows slightly post-Napoleonic uniforms, but the revised *Règlement* of the 1830s was essentially unchanged. Apart from the placing of his feet, each man is correctly executing one of the 25 movements of the manual of arms – (from left to right here) firing, taking a cartridge from his pouch, and ramming. (Philip Haythornthwaite Collection)

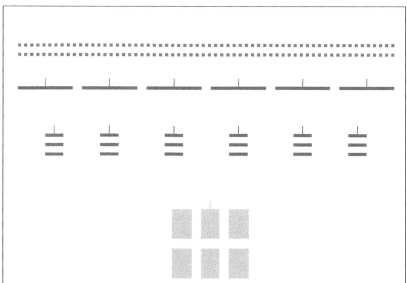

A Division on the battlefield. Under the Ancien Régime it had been common to draw up both first and second tactical lines in a deployed line three ranks deep. By 1792, however, it was more normal to deploy only the first line, keeping the second in battalion columns at 'deployment distance', i.e. with enough space between them to allow each battalion to deploy into line if required. The third line, if any, might be kept in an even heavier mass. This allowed units in the second and third lines to move more quickly to reinforce at need any point in the front line. Normally a screen of skirmishers would also be sent out forward of the front line.

(4,000 to 1,241); they launched some counter-attacks, but were finally forced to give way under the sheer weight of French numbers – and, to be fair, by the French persistence in renewing attacks after earlier ones had failed. Dumouriez was very much a product of the Ancien Régime and had served on De Broglie's staff as early as 1758, becoming a Chevalier of St Louis in 1763. In common with many of his colleagues and successors, he tried to run his army on classic lines, although he was often let down by the poor quality of his troops and the chaotic nature of the commissariat arrangements. He conquered Belgium in fine fashion, mainly because its Austrian garrison was so small; but his army immediately dissolved over the winter, and its remnants were defeated by the counter-attack at Neerwinden on 18 March 1793. Dumouriez emigrated in disgust at the lack of support he had received from the government in Paris, and he eventually died in Buckinghamshire, England, in 1823.

'REVOLUTIONARY WARFARE'

The defection of Dumouriez came as the last straw in a long series of emigrations by leading army and naval officers. It provoked a paroxysm of revolutionary fervour in Paris, where the politicians were starting to think that all their best commanders were royalists and traitors. They launched purges during which a total of 54 generals were executed and many more imprisoned, at least for a time (including Bonaparte, more than once). Also – of particular interest for the history of tactics – the civilian politicians laid down some new and 'democratic' military doctrines of their own, in an attempt to counteract the influence of the old royalist army. These doctrines were based on the idea that a new breed of democratic soldiers would be self-motivating and free to follow their own ideas, rather than having to be beaten into line by cruel drill sergeants. According to this analysis, the whole problem of maintaining morale and discipline in the army had been solved by the simple expedient of introducing a republican government in Paris.

Once the soldiers could be trusted to do the right thing, it was assumed they could then be released in large numbers, without any particular training, as unsupervised skirmishers. They could also dispense with all the complex minutiae of the *Règlement*, which was dismissed as 'Prussian drill' suitable only for mercenaries and slaves, but not for free citizens. All that these citizens had to do in battle was simply form up in a mass and charge forward fearlessly to crush the craven lackeys of autocrats and kings. In fact, the free citizens would not even need muskets and bayonets, which in any case were in short supply in 1793; they could surely make do with just pikes or scythes? The details of weapon technology were of no more importance to a free citizen than the details of mechanical drill; the only thing that really mattered was the revolutionary fervour of the soldiers.

This ideological fantasy clearly favoured the column attack with cold steel, rather than the evolutions in line to give fire as described in the *Règlement*. If the old military professionals preferred the latter, that

PASSAGE OF LINES
In the course of a battle the front-line battalions might run out of ammunition or become fatigued or otherwise unsettled, and a general might order a 'passage of the lines':

(A) The front-line units would reduce their frontage by ploying into columns of some sort – perhaps full battalion columns, perhaps with each platoon simply retiring behind its immediate neighbour.
(B) Meanwhile the second-line units would be advancing, also in columns, to provide gaps through which the front-line battalions could retreat. They would occupy the gaps left in the first line.
(C) When the second-line battalions arrived on the ground originally occupied by the first line, they would deploy into line to continue the battle.
(D) Meanwhile the original front-line units, covered by the new line, could fall back to regroup in the rear. In real battles the process was often, no doubt, a good deal less neat than this drill-ground solution, with the first line 'reducing its frontage' simply by running away in a formless crowd...

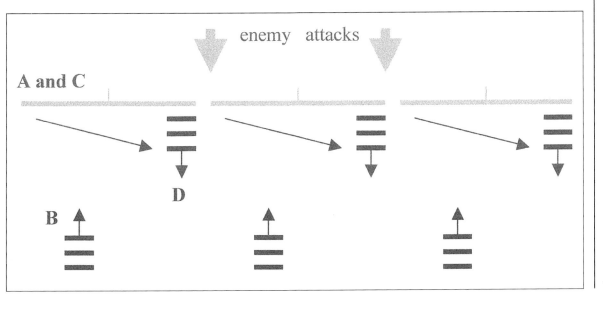

seemed reason enough to many civilian demagogues to favour the former. Thus, as early as 1793, the old arguments between enthusiasts for column and line, which Guibert and the *Règlement* were supposed to have resolved forever, seemed to have broken out anew; but in fact this was not quite the case. Under the Ancien Régime both sides of the debate had been assuming that the soldiers carrying out their preferred tactics would be well-trained professionals, whereas this new confrontation was between that ethos on one side, and a new ethos of 'inspired amateurism' on the other. In other words, at government level the debate was no longer about the practicalities of shock-versus-firepower formations at all, but had drifted off into a metaphysical quarrel about the spiritual virtues of scientific drill versus untutored enthusiasm.

In military terms it was obviously scientific drill, supported by old-fashioned discipline, that deserved to win every time. The highly trained majority of French generals continued to do everything they could to instruct their subordinates in the practicalities, especially by running training camps wherever large bodies of troops could be gathered together near the threatened frontiers. Some noted experts in infantry training were employed as drill-masters, such as Gen Hugues Meunier, who stressed movements in column to the Armée du Nord, and Gen Alexis Schauenbourg in Alsace, who preferred the line. Overall, fighting in line and with firepower remained the doctrine solidly favoured by the army, and to that extent the *Règlement* was well understood and widely disseminated.

The limitations of improvised armies

However, the intervention of the politicians now meant that no one could be unaware of the alternative doctrine, especially because the politicians made it their business to distribute their pamphlets,

An impressionistic panorama of the victorious French attack on the Piedmontese camp at Perulle in the Alps, 19 April 1793. The French are advancing up a steep hill and across a ridge in mountainous terrain. Skirmish screens are followed by columns, with what the present author imagines is a realistic level of disorganization in both cases, especially given the broken ground, which prevents regularity of drill movements. (After Rochu; Philip Haythornthwaite Collection)

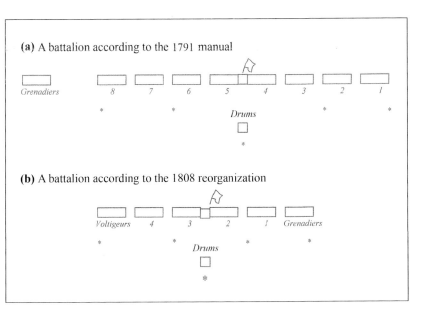

(a) A battalion according to the 1791 manual

Grenadiers 8 7 6 5 4 3 2 1

Drums

(b) A battalion according to the 1808 reorganization

Voltigeurs 4 3 2 1 Grenadiers

Drums

(a) The 1791 *Règlement* specified eight companies/platoons in the battalion line (with a frontage of 186 yards), plus a grenadier company that was normally detached. The troops were drawn up in three ranks, with the platoon commander (usually a captain) standing in the front rank on the right flank, with a sergeant behind him in the third rank. Two sergeants occupied comparable positions on the left flank of the 8th Platoon. Each platoon's two subaltern officers and four remaining sergeants formed a 'fourth rank' behind it, to repeat orders and 'persuade' the men to remain in their places. There was a 'fifth rank' 8 paces behind them (shown here by asterisks), consisting of a 'guide' behind each flank of the battalion to help monitor adjustments, with the mounted adjutant and adjutant-major spaced between them. At the centre of the line stood the colour party of nine NCOs in three ranks, with the flag in the front rank. The drums from all platoons (a total of 18 or 27) collected in a group 15 paces behind the colour party. Finally, the mounted battalion commander was posted 20 paces behind the flag, with an overview of the whole formation.

(b) The 1808 reorganization reduced the battalion to six companies/platoons, including one each of grenadiers and voltigeurs. Otherwise the arrangements were essentially as in 1791, although each platoon was now supposed to be somewhat bigger, and the frontage of the battalion would be 171 yards.

newspapers and other propaganda as widely as possible around the armies.[2] This was reinforced by the acid fact that although many of the first revolutionary recruits were admirably enthusiastic republicans who were good at learning tactics, many of the later drafts were reluctant conscripts who were tactically unreliable – they were, in short, incapable of adhering to the *Règlement* for very long in a battle. The French infantry's record in the field during the Revolutionary Wars is notably peppered with a series of the most shameful routs and panics which made formal drill quite impossible.

Perhaps the worst panics occurred when large formations of French infantry, even in square, were attacked by well-trained Allied regular cavalry, even in relatively small numbers. This happened at Avesnes le Sec on 12 September and Lannoy on 28 October 1793; at Catillon on 17 April 1794, Villers en Cauchies on 24 April, Beaumont on 26 April, Willems on 10 May, and elsewhere.[3] The shakiness of the infantry was habitually made worse in the face of enemy cavalry because the French at this period had very few cavalry of their own, and what they did have was rarely well trained. Nor was the Revolutionary infantry immune from panics when it faced only enemy infantry. One example among many came at Pirmasens on 14 September 1793, where the French found themselves milling around in a narrow valley under Prussian fire from the heights above.

The key element was the difference in unit cohesion and discipline between the two sides. Professor John Lynn has put forward a compelling thesis that the unquestionable professionalism of most French generals in the 1790s was rapidly 'trickled down' to the rank and file by a rigid regime of drill camps and intensive training.[4] French troops in the main armies were already forming up in all the regulation tactical formations as early as 1792, so they cannot be dismissed as simply 'armed mobs'. That description would be highly appropriate for

[2] John Lynn, *Bayonets of the Republic*, Ch 6, 'The political education of the Armée du Nord'
[3] See my *Art of War of Revolutionary France*, p.187
[4] John Lynn, *Bayonets of the Republic*, passim but especially Ch 11, 'Line and column on the battlefield'

Column and line in action at Thionville, 16 October 1792. A French column from the left appears to be driving off the grenadiers covering the flank of an Austrian line, which is engaged in a firefight with a French line. The full range of drill-book manoeuvres were already in use on the battlefields of this early period, although it would take time for the French troops to gain experience, confidence and tactical cohesion. (After Lecomte; Philip Haythornthwaite Collection)

many of the internal armies, political lynching-columns and bandit gangs that roamed France during the 'Terror' of 1793–94, but it does not quite fit the 'real' armies operating on the frontiers of the state.[5]

These 'real' armies nevertheless fell far short of the military efficiency that was found in the long-service professional forces of the Ancien Régime. They lacked the necessary experience and long period of socialization into military ways that were the hallmark of true regulars. They were still essentially improvised armies of conscripts, learning their trade in an ever-changing and extremely dangerous environment, without the benefit of a strong corps of long-service non-commissioned officers. Those who managed to survive the war of the First Coalition would doubtless progress to become genuine veterans or, as Bonaparte would call them, *grognards* ('grumblers'), but in 1792–97 very few of them could yet claim that status.

Any given French army might well start its battle in formal array, and might at first deliver massed volleys according to the *Règlement*. But the problem was that it could not usually manage to maintain regularity for very long at key points where the pressure became intense. Even if it was not chased away, the formed front line might degenerate into what was effectively a skirmish line. Attempts might then be made to push forward columns from the rear which, if their attacks did not succeed, would themselves degenerate into formless blobs. Such battles could continue for a long time in an indecisive manner, with the artillery often saving the infantry from a worse fate.

---

[5] See Richard Cobb, *Les armées révolutionnaires*, 2 vols, Paris 1961–66; English translation as *The People's Armies*, Yale, London 1987

The enemy's regular forces were often outnumbered by the revolutionary masses. They could stand in line and defend themselves very well, but were frequently unable to finish off the battle by a general offensive. At the decisive battle of Fleurus on 26 June 1794 the Austrians even began by launching a series of assaults which, after a very hard-fought day, held the French to at least a draw. However, the Austrian commander then consulted his secret political orders and realized that he had no need to fight at all. Tired of the game, he retreated without being forced to do so. (It transpired that the core Austrian war aim was to allow the French to capture Belgium so that the Austrians – through the arcane workings of 18th-century diplomatic logic – would be awarded Bavaria as compensation. Oddly, in the event they weren't.)

To a French general in this period it must often have seemed that the best thing to do was to stand on the defensive, so that his unreliable troops would hardly have to manoeuvre at all in the presence of the enemy. Guibert himself had said that even professional soldiers would be thrown into a state of crisis as soon as they tried to perform changes of formation under close-range fire; so what hope was there for the dubious conscript hordes who were thrown into the field in 1793? But there were some dire personal examples to give such generals pause. General le Flers was executed for winning a splendid defensive victory against a numerically superior (especially in cavalry) Spanish regular army outside Perpignan on 17 July 1793. His problem was that his ultra-politicized masters reasoned that if he was capable of beating off the enemy by standing in line, then he could just as easily have destroyed them totally by launching a counter-attack. It was his failure to 'manoeuvre' that cost him his life, even though he had been professionally aware that any attempt to do so would have been fatal not only to his improvised army, but also to the whole French position in the eastern Pyrenees.

There were deep political reasons, ultimately of a financial nature, why French generals were expected to fight on the offensive, but during the Revolutionary Wars they did not possess armies that were capable of winning clean and decisive battles of manoeuvre. Instead, the battles tended to be messy attritional affairs, with blobs of infantry and unorganized skirmish lines being the main tactical formations. It was often merely the dogged persistence of the French, and their ability to continue reinforcing the front line (with or without a formal 'passage of lines') that won the day.

General Count Philippe-Guillaume Duhesme (1766–1815) at the battle of Diersheim, 20 April 1797; to encourage his men he picked up a drum from a fallen drummer and beat it with his sword pommel. Duhesme, a highly experienced tactician, would eventually be killed at Waterloo. His lasting monument was a treatise on light infantry, which would remain a classic through much of the 19th century. (After Perrigeon; Philip Haythornthwaite Collection)

A French skirmisher takes cartridges from the pouch of his fallen comrade, in order to carry on the fight. This was obviously sensible; but it was also commonplace for soldiers on the battlefield to loot the packs and pockets of their own, as well as enemy casualties. (Philip Haythornthwaite Collection)

Skirmishers

The inner story of skirmishers in this period has to be described as controversial, or even murky.

According to some authorities, they were an overwhelming 'secret weapon' on the battlefield. They used cover and could take time over each aimed shot, rather than having to fire without aiming on a word of command. For example, the French victory over a force of Hessians and Hanoverians at Hondeschoote on 6–8 September 1793 has been attributed entirely to the attritional effect of skirmish fire. Command volleys fired by outnumbered regular troops could never effectively chase away a dispersed swarm or 'cloud' of skirmishers, any more than a fly swat can hope to kill more than one fly at a time. Yet other authorities regard them as no more than 'auxiliaries', who might have had some part to play in softening up the enemy, but who could never swing the result of a battle on their own. Especially when the skirmishers were untrained for their task, they would be unable to shoot straight or maintain pressure on the enemy in any sustained way.

The best-known French theorist of skirmishing was General Count Philippe-Guillaume Duhesme (1766–1815), who had already commanded a brigade in the Armée du Nord in 1793–94, when he was wounded several times. He later served with distinction as a Division commander on the Rhine, in Italy, and later still in Catalonia, although he was disgraced and reinstated three times during that period (apparently his political ideas were too democratic for the military dictator he served). Eventually he fought through 1813–15 with the Grand Armée, and fell mortally wounded at Plancenoit during the battle of Waterloo. It would be hard to think of anyone who saw more of these wars at the tactical level than Duhesme, although he never quite found that elusive baton in his knapsack.

Duhesme made his first mark on tactical theory in the Boulogne camp of 1805, when he issued comprehensive instructions for skirmishing to his Division. His famous book, *Essai historique sur l'infanterie légère,* appeared in 1814, and would become highly influential during the decades that followed, although obviously it appeared too late to exert any significant influence upon the Napoleonic Wars themselves. What he said in its pages was basically that during the early Revolutionary days there had often been formless masses – *'grandes bandes'* – of untrained skirmishers; but that as time went on there had been an increasing realization that truly effective skirmishers required good training. In particular, there was a need to keep back a formed reserve behind each skirmish line, upon which the dispersed troops could fall back if they were counter-attacked. During the early days there were admittedly some regiments that attempted to give such training, and some specialists in the art did indeed exist. We might add that one of them, Francis de Rottenburg (1757–1832), emigrated to Britain to write manuals, and in the early 1800s it was he who inspired the (perhaps over-celebrated) training of the light regiments at Shorncliffe that would be commanded by Sir John Moore. Nevertheless, it seems to be true that only relatively few of the French skirmishers in the period 1792–1815 did in fact enjoy anything like a proper training régime for the particular skills they required.

This interpretation has sometimes been disputed. Some authorities have claimed that Duhesme's alleged *grandes bandes* did not exist, and that everything was done with much more training, regularity and deliberation than he reported. Sometimes 64 men, 100 men, or one or even two platoons per battalion might be sent forward to skirmish, or perhaps one entire battalion per brigade. The numbers might vary according to the

In the absence of an army-wide drill manual for skirmishing, there were many ways to construct a skirmish line. Sometimes the troops in the front line simply shook out into dispersed order on their own initiative, as a response to broken ground, or the awkwardness of firing and reloading in the 'touch of elbows' proximity demanded for close order. This was sometimes called 'skirmishing by *grandes bandes*' or big crowds, and might involve any number of men from a platoon to a brigade. If skirmishing was premeditated by a unit specifically trained for the role, two principles were normally observed. Firstly, skirmishers would act in pairs, loading and firing alternately so that one musket was always ready to fire. Secondly, some men would always be held back in close order behind the skirmishers, so that the dispersed pairs could fall back and rally upon them in case of need.

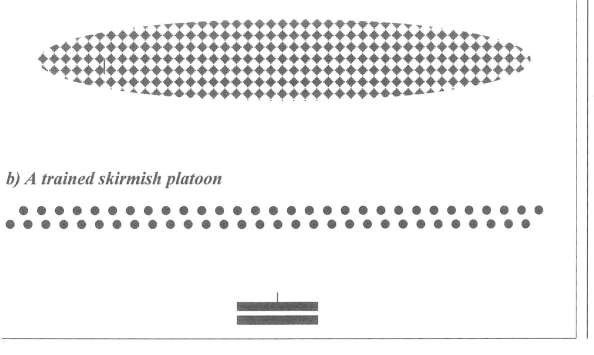

a) A 'Grande Bande'

b) A trained skirmish platoon

ABOVE **French columns of platoons (background) advancing against an Austrian skirmish screen and battery. The nearer of the two battalions has full deployment intervals between its platoons, and its grenadiers (note tall bearskins) in the van. The background battalion is 'closed', with intervals too small to allow platoons to wheel through 90 degrees into a fully deployed line. (Anne S.K.Brown Library, Providence, RI)**

RIGHT **A diagram showing the basic idea of a 1796 three-battalion demi-brigade arranged in an *ordre mixte*: the central battalion is fully deployed in line, and the other two are placed in column on its flanks. The columns might be by platoon or by division, giving the demi-brigade a total frontage to give fire of either ten or 12 platoons. Columns might be 'open' or 'closed' depending upon the perceived threats to the flanks: the former allowed platoons to wheel quickly outwards into a continuous line to face infantry, while the latter might be best for forming a battalion square against cavalry.**

personal ideas of the commander on the spot or the training each unit had received. There is certainly plenty of evidence that this type of approach was often used – but that does not mean that there were no *grandes bandes* on many other occasions too.

It seems that the two systems co-existed simultaneously. It is also clear that for well over a decade enemy troops were often very impressed by the numbers and firepower of their skirmishing opponents, and on a few occasions they reported that the French went one step further and actually launched bayonet assaults in open order. This 'skirmish charge' was not in any manual, and in theory it was an extremely stupid thing to attempt against a formed line. In the heat of battle, however, it might occasionally be appropriate if the enemy was in disorder and the French skirmishers were numerous and rampant. One example is Suchet's attack on a redoubt at Montserrat on 25 July 1811, where his voltigeurs, supported by just two formed companies of grenadiers, were able to infiltrate behind the Spanish.

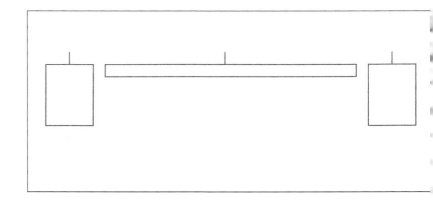

FROM THE 'TERROR' TO THE *COUP* OF BRUMAIRE

If skirmish training became increasingly regularized as the 1790s progressed, the same could also be said of many other parts of the French battlefield. Above all, the troops who had survived the multiple crises of 1792–94 had necessarily, by that very fact, grown in experience and understanding of what they might expect to encounter in combat. They had evolved from 'greenhorn' status into veterans; and the same was even more true of their officers.

Many of the political popinjays were weeded out, while the brilliant young thrusters came to the fore. By the time Bonaparte launched his famous offensive into Italy in 1796, a high proportion of his subordinates were already battle-hardened, and 'professional' in the sense that they knew what they were doing in military terms. He was quick to shower these men with riches in return for their services, cynically diverting their loyalty to himself personally and away from the elected government, which he increasingly seemed confident enough to disregard. For example, Bonaparte levied taxes on six French *départements* close to the Italian frontier, without any authority to do so; equally, he made up his own foreign policy in Italy without reference to Paris, and often defined his tactical aims by the amount of booty that could be collected. Thus it came about that, although Italy had been rich and Bonaparte's army had been poor at the start of the 1796 campaign, by the end of it that situation had largely been reversed.

Meanwhile, a number of tactical innovations were under way. The idea of massing artillery, especially exploiting the extra mobility of horse artillery, was starting to become well understood; and the French had a distinct advantage over their enemies by virtue of the superior mobility of their Gribeauval-designed guns. Even the cavalry was gradually

Bonaparte's innovative use of *l'ordre mixte* at the crossing of the Taglimento, 16 March 1797. Other than skirmishing, it did not have to prove itself in combat on that occasion; and although it did reappear from time to time thereafter, it is unclear whether or not it was as important as some have claimed.
(A) Three demi-brigades in *ordre mixte,* side by side. Ahead of them, cavalry (B) guard the flanks of a thick skirmish screen (C) composed of a whole demi-brigade of light infantry, which is supported behind each flank by a composite battalion of grenadier platoons (D) detached from their parent units.

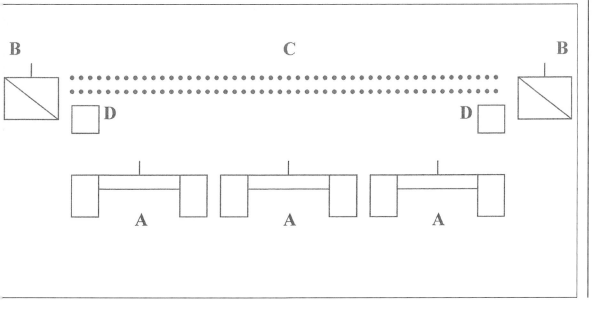

A platoon in three ranks advancing with muskets shouldered, apparently as a rearward fraction of an open column – i.e. with the front-to-back interval between each platoon sufficiently wide to allow deployment to the flank by a simple wheel of each platoon. At centre, note the veteran sergeant sporting three service chevrons on his left upper sleeve. Behind him, the artist has shown realistically the difficulty of keeping alignment while advancing over ground strewn with the dead and dying. (After Raffet; Philip Haythornthwaite Collection)

improving in both quality and quantity, and the whole idea of the 'all-arms battle' was gaining momentum. In particular, the infantry was becoming more supple in its evolution, with increasingly resilient and flexible formations. The Division had already established itself as a unit of manoeuvre: but now the Army Corps was beginning to be seen as an efficient way to combine the action of several Divisions, and all their supporting arms, under the hand of a single commander.

The commanders themselves were apparently still exercised by *les grandes querelles* as between the column and the line. Despite the *Règlement* of 1791 there never does seem to have been a universal consensus on which formations were best in battle. Some commanders still liked to attack in line, according to the classic model. Others preferred to attack in column since, even if it did not break through cleanly, or even deploy cleanly into a regulation firing line, it could still be expected to break down into some sort of ragged firing line or thick skirmish line rather than running away. This in itself could wear down the enemy by musketry, after which a regular 'passage of lines' by its reserves could replace it with fresh troops who could finish off the action.

L'ordre mixte

In his Italian campaign Bonaparte lodged a rather dubious claim to tactical originality when he favoured the *ordre mixte* ('composite order'), although in fact it had already – like so many other things – been described by Guibert. It was a sort of compromise between column and line. In a *demi-brigade* of three battalions there might typically be a central battalion deployed in line to give fire, with another one on each flank in column, to give solidity in case of cavalry attack. These flanking battalions could turn outwards – or even form square – in case of need, thereby protecting from cavalry the thinner line that lay between them. The classic prototype is often cited as the crossing of the Tagliamento on 16 March 1797, then of the Isonzo three days later.

In later battles many variations of this arrangement were attempted, all the way down to Macdonald's 'monstrous column' at Wagram (see Plate F); this was a huge and lop-sided application of the same principle, which has sometimes even been interpreted as a giant 'square against cavalry' comparable to Suchet's Division at Jena (though the latter was, unlike Macdonald's formation, fully closed off). A grotesque variation came at Friedland, where Ney's Corps had one Division all in line and the other all in column. But also at Friedland, Victor's Division used the highly conventional arrangement of a skirmish line followed by a deployed line, followed by a line of columns towards the flanks, followed by a brigade mass (see diagram on page 12). If viewed in a certain light, this might itself perhaps be seen as a sort of *ordre mixte*, but it is stretching the definition.

In practice, however, the whole idea of *l'ordre mixte* smacked of an over-theoretical solution. If there was a cavalry threat, the central line might be seen as too thin, whereas if there were an artillery threat, the columns on the flanks would be too vulnerable. It is noticeable that although Bonaparte continued to advocate *l'ordre mixte* throughout his wars, rather few of his subordinates seem to have adopted it when not directly under his eye. In his memoirs (which appeared after Bonaparte was safely dead), Marshal Marmont was openly critical of his command of infantry tactics. Both of them had been trained as gunners, but Marmont believed that he understood infantry much better than his master.

Line and column in the attack

The preferred formation for defence was always the deployed line, covered by skirmishers, artillery, and preferably cavalry too, with columns held in reserve. But when it comes to the attack, the picture is much cloudier. When the present author analysed a sample of some 226 French infantry attacks from the whole period 1792–1815, he found the formations used were as shown in the panel on page 24.[6] The sample was taken from a selection of the readily available accounts of combat, which doubtless skewed them unduly towards English-language sources and so, by extension, towards battles between the French and the British, which form about a quarter of the sample.

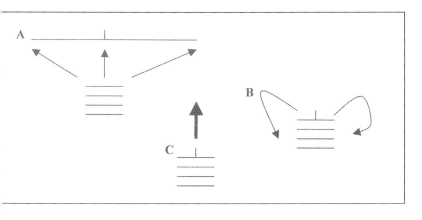

ASSAULT FORMATIONS
It was conventional wisdom that a battalion attack in column was supposed to deploy into line – (A) – to beat down the enemy by fire before driving him back. However, if the deployment was left too late and the enemy were resolute, the battalion would be thrown back in confusion – (B) – and very vulnerable to counter-attack, as happened on many occasions when facing British infantry. There were also occasions, e.g. when facing weak opponents or on very confined ground, when a commander would wish to remain in column – (C) – without making any attempt to deploy, simply pushing on by sheer force of 'shock'.

mpare John Lynn, *Bayonets of the Republic*, p.287 & ff, 'Tables concerning tactical practice', which cover the Armée du rd in the early 1790s. They are reported in George Nafziger, *Imperial Bayonets*, pp.162–3

The idea of an echelon attack was to concentrate one's hardest-hitting unit against a perceived weak spot in the enemy line, whether a flank or any other weakly held section. If this first encounter went well, the second unit, arriving later, would have an easier time, and so on along the line; with luck, the rearmost echelons would not need to engage at all. In some cases the echelons would not all march directly ahead, as here, but would follow the first towards the key point, marching in an oblique direction.

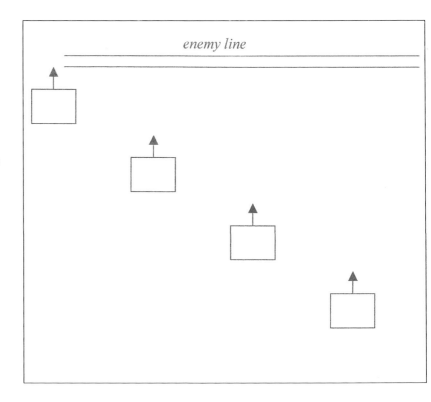

Perhaps surprisingly, there was an overwhelming preponderance of attacks in column as opposed to the more regulation line or *l'ordre mixte*. However, a definitional difficulty lies behind these figures, since according to the official consensus around 1791, it was seen as normal to begin an advance in column and then to deploy into line when closer to the enemy. A significant proportion of attacks that are recorded here as being in 'column' doubtless managed to perform this manoeuvre successfully. Yet very many of them must have failed to achieve it. British eyewitness accounts from the Peninsula often mention attempts to move from column into line that were shot down or otherwise aborted before they could be completed. This is exactly what had already happened at Pirmasens against the Prussians in 1793, and in many other battles.

Then again, there were also many occasions on which French tacticians felt they did not have to deploy into line at all, often because the frontage available was exceptionally narrow. In classic theory the column had always been the recommended formation for 'affairs of posts', such as the storming of a breach in a fortress wall, and in the sample studied above it turns out that as many as 65 per cent of the 226 attacks were launched over rough or narrow ground.

Analysis of French infantry attacks, 1792–1815

Total sample	226 attacks
In column	174 (78% of total sample)
In line	30 (13%)
In *ordre mixte*	19 (8%)
In skirmish order	3 (1%)

This sample includes 15 attacks (6%) in echelon; 148 (65%) on rough or narrow ground; and 58 (26%) against British troops.

Street-fighting at Essling,
21–22 May 1809: this impression
is probably fairly realistic. In
such circumstances – with
the 'battlefield' broken up by
buildings, and short fields of
fire – there was never any
chance of 'regularity' in the way
men fought. It was notoriously
difficult to reload while prone
or sitting, as shown here.
(After de Myrbach; Philip
Haythornthwaite Collection)

However, it does seem that French column attacks would sometimes remain undeployed simply because the quality of the opposition seemed sufficiently low. On such occasions generals believed that they could steamroller their opponents purely by the speed and cohesion of a mass attack, without the need to resort to tactical niceties. We might thus identify one set of tactics to be used against 'good' enemies, and a quite different, and lazier one to be used against 'poor' enemies. We can agree with authorities such as James Arnold who point out that French attacks were often intended to be deployed into line.[7] However, the evidence seems to show that this intention was often compromised in practice (see the Peninsular War, below).

One finding of interest is that 6 per cent of the attacks in this sample were made in echelons, regardless of whether each individual echelon was deployed in column, line or *ordre mixte*. The echelon attack had been a hallmark of the tactics of Frederick the Great, and was deeply embedded in classic military theory. It would be taken up by a number of French theorists during the Napoleonic era, most notably Marshal Ney in his writings of 1805. The basic idea was to deliver a succession of blows along the enemy's line, with hopefully the heaviest and most disruptive arriving first against a vulnerable point such as an open flank.

The need for speed was also gaining currency, regardless of the formation in which an attack was conducted. The basic step was laid down as the *pas de charge* of 120 paces (each of 26in) per minute, which totalled 260ft (or 87 yards) per minute. This was considerably faster than many of the tactical systems seen under the Ancien Régime, although obviously it would always be highly variable in practice, depending on

---

[7] See his article 'Column versus line in the Napoleonic Wars. A reappraisal'

the terrain. A number of French tacticians now also liked to stress the jog, or *pas de course* of 200 paces or more per minute, which made 433ft (or 144 yards).[8] The idea was to cross the 'beaten ground' as fast as possible, thereby limiting the number of volleys that the enemy could fire before the attackers came to close quarters. There is certainly plenty of evidence to show that French infantry officers led from the front, sometimes in a highly sacrificial manner, and tried to do all they could to encourage their men to press forward without halting or hesitating.

Linked to this was the idea of attacking without firing at all. This was already a common practice in the storming of fortresses, since it was found that as soon as the soldiers opened fire their forward momentum would stop. But now the same principle was extended to attacks in open battle; some commanders even told their men not to load their muskets before an attack, or at least not to put priming powder into the pans of their flintlocks.

Defensive tactics

When it came to defence, a number of other tactics apart from the straightforward line formation were now being accepted as standard. The arrangement for the defence of villages, for example, relied on skirmishers dispersed and barricaded in the village itself, supported by formed columns held in reserve to the rear, outside the reach of enemy artillery. If the enemy made progress in his attack, the reserve columns would counter-attack to clear them out of the village and restore the original situation. Examples can be found in Brune's defence of Bergen, 19 September to

A battalion 'square' – in reality a rectangle – as it was supposed to be formed after the re-organization of February 1808 reduced the battalion to six platoons. This came to be known as the *carré d'Egypte*, since in the popular mind Egypt was vaguely associated with forming squares against cavalry. In fact, of course, those formed in Egypt involved entire Divisions rather than single battalions (see Plate C). Before 1808 the eight platoons of each battalion could form a true, symmetrical square.

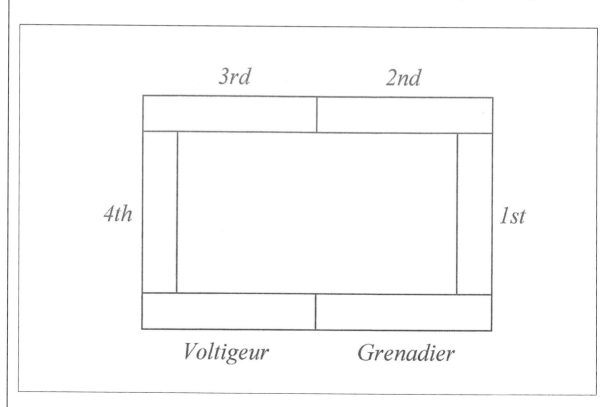

[8] See George Nafziger, *Imperial Bayonets*, pp.55–57, for further details

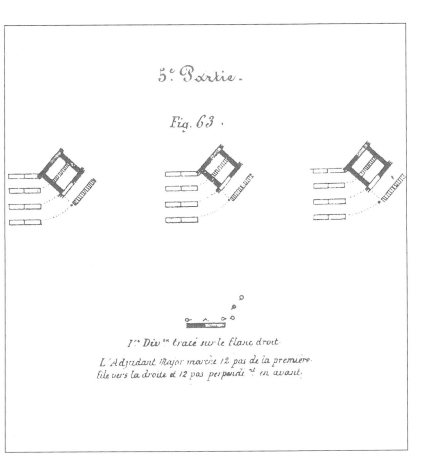

5.ᵉ Partie.

Fig. 63.

1.ᵉ Div.ⁿ tracé sur le flanc droit.

L'Adjudant Major marche 12 pas de la première file vers la droite et 12 pas perpend.ᵗ en avant.

There were many different ways to form a battalion square, depending on the original formation and many other factors. In this case three battalions of eight platoons, each in close column of divisions, wheel successively to their right front. They then form a line of squares at 45° to the original direction of march, with the leading corners facing the enemy, so that fire from any face of a square would miss the other squares. Another method of forming square from column of divisions is illustrated on Plate E, inset 3.

6 October 1799 (see Plate D), or Gardanne's at Marengo. Often the enemy might then renew his assault, so the whole cycle would begin again. It might continue all day, and we often hear of battles in which particular villages changed hands, backwards and forwards, several times.

Another defensive measure that was increasingly being mastered by French tacticians was the square against cavalry. There had been training in this difficult manoeuvre since 1791, with both battalion and brigade (or even bigger) squares being practised. But now the infantry was starting to have more confidence in their efficacy, as the massed panics of the early years receded into the past and their own cavalry supports gradually grew in competence. Apart from anything else, the enclosed terrain in Italy was often less suitable for Austrian cavalry than the plains of Belgium had been.

When Bonaparte embarked on his ill-judged Egyptian campaign his troops encountered a different type of enemy horseman, in the shape of the Mamelukes. These were ferocious warriors, born to the saddle, but lacking any sort of regular drill. They fought as individuals, and they were found to be practically powerless if the French infantry maintained close cohesion and steadiness in large squares, each of a whole Division. These formations became known as *les carrés d'Egypte* ('Egyptian squares'), and they would become a reference point for anti-cavalry tactics among the *grognards* ever afterwards (see Plate C). Confusingly, however, the rectangular battalion 'square' that was introduced after the reduction of the battalion to six platoons/companies under the reorganization of 1808 would also be referred to as a *carré d'Egypte*.

Corner of a Consular Guard square at Marengo, 14 June 1800; the men are firing at will, three deep. The dead cuirassier indicates that they are fighting off cavalry, although in reality it was often the bayonets rather than the fire of an infantry square that posed the biggest problem for horses. Note the man at the extreme corner of the square, cocking his weapon in exactly the correct official posture for the 18th drill movement ('Make ready your arms') in the loading and firing sequence. (After Raffet; Philip Haythornthwaite Collection)

LA GRANDE ARMÉE

When Bonaparte returned from Egypt in 1799, his first thought was to overthrow the elected government in the *coup d'état* of Brumaire, thereby effectively suppressing democracy in France for half a century (and arguably, until 1871). In the shorter term, his second thought was to perpetuate the remorseless series of wars of aggression which had begun in 1792, and which he would continue until 1815.

Despite having shamefully abandoned his élite veteran troops in Egypt, he was nevertheless able to scrape together a surprisingly combat-worthy force for the Marengo campaign of 1800. By this time the numerically strong French armies were sufficiently battered by both success and failure to contain a wide selection of experienced men at every rank. At Marengo they displayed a reassuringly high level of competence in all-arms tactics, including the integration of artillery and cavalry support for the infantry. General Desaix attacked in three echelons, each of a demi-brigade in some form of *ordre mixte*, which were able to halt the enemy's advance by their fire, although their own counter-charge was then also halted by fire. General Monnier attacked with two demi-brigades in a line of battalion 'open columns of division'; after breaking the enemy infantry, the intervals of this open column allowed companies to wheel to form square against cavalry. All this showed that the First Consul's troops were tactically efficient, and that they could help form the basis of an army for the future.

The Boulogne camp, 1804–05

This army would be *la Grande Armée*, which was shaped and trained in the great Boulogne camp of 1804–05. (La Grande Armée was officially so named on 29 August 1805, although the name already had resonance: it had been used loosely for the Armée du Nord in the early 1790s.)

The army was originally planned as a force of well over 100,000 men to invade south-east England, and it conducted extensive training for embarkation on to the large flotilla of transports and warships that was specially collected for the task. A powerful line of coastal batteries was also built to beat off interventions by the Royal Navy. However, the real significance of the new Grande Armée was considerably greater than that, and in the event it was never called upon to perform amphibious operations any more ambitious than river crossings. Its prolonged training in large-unit drill turned out to be far more significant than its nautical training – it perfected the art of manoeuvre on land rather than transport by sea.

The creation of the Grande Armée coincided with the inauguration of the Empire, and all the many lavish ceremonies (and fancy gold-encrusted uniforms) that went with it. Bonaparte was determined to reverse the Revolution and lure back the émigré noblemen whose military talents had been lost to France during the early 1790s. He handed out medals, titles, estates and all the other trappings of nobility on an industrial scale. In particular he reinstated the Marshalate, which the Revolution had abolished, as a means of marking out a few favoured generals as the Emperor's foremost lieutenants, who would be capable of acting independently of his close personal supervision. They became the natural candidates to command the Army Corps that were now being regularized and reorganized at Boulogne.

Each Corps was intended to manoeuvre as an autonomous formation, with its own separate aims. In some cases a single Corps was enough to control a province or even a whole country (with the consequence that more than a few of the marshals soon developed ambitions to become princes and kings in their own right). In other cases a group of Corps would manoeuvre in generally the same direction, in a broad fan covering a total frontage of perhaps 200km (125 miles). Then, at a word of command from Imperial Headquarters, the fan would snap shut, and all would concentrate together on a single battlefield, with a total frontage of perhaps 10km (6 miles). It was this flexibility which gave the French a distinct operational advantage over their opponents for several years.

Another result of the establishment of the Empire was that it further cemented the loyalties of the troops directly to Bonaparte's own person. He often gloated that the glory and glitter of his pageants could buy the heart of even the most gnarled and cynical old soldier. Perhaps more importantly, he was now unambiguously both the

Marshal Michel Ney, Duke of Elchingen, was one of Bonaparte's leading tacticians. Although he would gain a reputation for wild recklessness on the field, in the Boulogne camp of 1805 he revealed the more reflective side of his personality, being responsible for an elaborate set of tactical instructions which stressed the use of battalion columns. (After Tietze and Gerard; Philip Haythornthwaite Collection)

A drum major of the Imperial Guard at the head of a corps of drums (see also Plate H). It is alleged that the drum major shown in this picture is modelled on the brave Lt Sénot, who led the Guard band under the Directory, the Consulate and the Empire; he was wounded at Leipzig (1813), but continued to serve until Waterloo in 1815. (After Colin and Raffet; Philip Haythornthwaite Collection)

head of state and the commander of the army in the field, in a way that could not be said of the British King George III, the Austrian Emperor Francis I, the Prussian King Frederick William III or Czar Alexander I. This factor gave a powerful boost to the 'team spirit' of the Grande Armée, which in turn solidified its tactical cohesion – especially when it was winning.

The troops' tactical cohesion was further solidified at Boulogne by the mere fact of living together in one place in the same large units, and with the same officers and NCOs who would lead them on campaign. The bivouacs they built for themselves also gave a much better impression of life in the field than dank masonry barrack blocks scattered around a variety of soulless garrison towns ever could. Beyond that, the frequent field days and drill exercises implanted order, discipline and correct methods that would soon prove to be invaluable on the battlefield. The use of similar camps had already been well known to the generals of the early 1790s; but the army that emerged from Boulogne was no longer a hesitant collection of conscripts whose formations were likely to dissolve under pressure. It was a tough and a professional army in every meaningful sense.

In the Boulogne camp there was also a flurry of intellectual activity and publishing, on the part of senior officers, that might put many other armies to shame. Several of the Corps, Division and even regimental commanders issued manuals for the tactics of their men, although there was no official new army-wide manual. Duhesme's drills for skirmishing by his Division have already been mentioned; now Marshal Michel Ney also issued a voluminous 'instruction' on tactics for his Corps (presented in Vol II of his memoirs); Gen Meunier published his *Dissertation sur l'ordonnance d'infanterie*, and there were others. One of Ney's aides-de-camp, Chef de bataillon Antoine-Henri de Jomini, had already just published a *traité des grandes opérations* in 1803, and he would quickly become the most influential military writer in the world for at least the next 60 years. (During that time Jomini eclipsed even Karl von Clausewitz, who was by far his intellectual superior, until literary opinion began to turn towards the latter as a result of certain non-literary events at Sedan on 1–3 September 1870.)

It would be incorrect to say that all parts of the army camped around Boulogne learned exactly the same tactics there, since each commander had his own personal ideas about an infinity of details; but at least there were a few common themes. The first was that remorseless training in drill (which in those days amounted to much the same thing as tactics) was essential for everyone at every rank. The second was that the column was the real key to battle-handling. As Ney put it, 'The march and evolutions of columns form the essential part of tactics' – although he would certainly have added that these evolutions should include deployments into line whenever they were required. Marshal Louis-Nicolas Davout seems to have agreed with Ney's analysis. Both of them were consummate tacticians, as they had already demonstrated many times before Boulogne, and would continue to do thereafter. The wily Marshal Nicolas Soult was perhaps somewhat less adept at minor tactics; at Boulogne his idea of a 'column' was to build an elaborate stone one in honour of his Emperor (which may still be inspected today on the site of his camp).

The third consensus that was forming among prominent tacticians by 1804–05, which many of them had already realized years earlier, was that the *Règlement* of 1791 needed to be simplified. The problem, as always, was that there were as many conflicting opinions as to exactly how it should be simplified as there were experts in the field. The perceived need seems to have been a reduction of pedantry, from which the *Règlement* could emerge as a set of essential but simple drills that could easily be learned. The list did not extend very much further than the march in line and column (including how to narrow frontages when obstacles were encountered); a few simple ways to change from one to the other, or back again; and, of course, forming square against cavalry.

This need for simplification (though some would say that Ney's *Instruction* was far from simple) is a theme that would resonate not only through the literature of the 1800s, but also through that of the following generation, until the *Règlement* was finally revised in 1831. Nor was it confined to the officers of the Boulogne camp, since other skilled tacticians who were not present at Boulogne would often echo it. An outstanding example is Laurent Gouvion St Cyr, who had gained a

An example of the price of 'sacrificial leadership' on the field: the monument to Gen Maximilien-Sébastien Foy's fourteenth wound, which he sustained at the battle of Orthez on 27 February 1814, from British shellfire. Monuments to the wounded are extraordinarily rare when compared to the vast numbers dedicated to the dead; in Foy's case it presumably owes a great deal to his popularity as a liberal agitator against the restored Bourbon monarchy in 1814. Tens of thousands of French officers, of every rank right up to the occasional marshal, paid a heavy and even fatal price for leading from the front in a tactical role. (Author's collection)

A (slightly post-Napoleonic) mounted adjutant supervising from the rear the firing line of the half-battalion for which he is responsible in action. From his elevated position in the saddle he has a clear view not only of the firing ranks, but also of the colour party at the centre front; of the guides off to each side of him, who are responsible for indicating alignments; of the drum major a few paces behind him, through whom he can transmit orders; and of the battalion commander, behind the drums, from whom all orders ultimately originate. (Philip Haythornthwaite Collection)

reputation as a cold, calculating, tactical 'chess-player' during his Rhine campaigns of the 1790s. He was never very impressed with Bonaparte, which delayed his promotion to marshal until 1812; but his memoirs show that his thinking was no less advanced than that of the other leading tacticians of his day.

High tide, 1805–07

When the Grande Armée marched out of Boulogne in the autumn of 1805 it was not only its generals who possessed a sophisticated understanding of tactics, as had too often been the case in the early 1790s. This time it was the entire army, right down to the last drummer boy, who knew all the drills; and they proved it, all the way down the Danube to Austerlitz in that year, and through Jena to Berlin in 1806. Notwithstanding the hysterical excesses of Bonaparte's idolators, then and since, this episode in his profligate campaigning life certainly demands attention.

The Ulm campaign (finally won on the same day that the naval battle of Trafalgar was lost) passed off almost without serious combat. There was, however, an interesting confrontation at Hasslach when Gen Pierre Dupont (a highly successful tactician, at least until he arrived at Baílen in 1808) formed up his three infantry regiments in a single line (i.e. without a second line in reserve, apart from some dragoons), and beat off the Austrians. It was very daring to fight without a reserve line in rear, but it paid off.

(continued on page 41)

A

B

WATTIGNIES, 15 October 1793
See text commentary for details

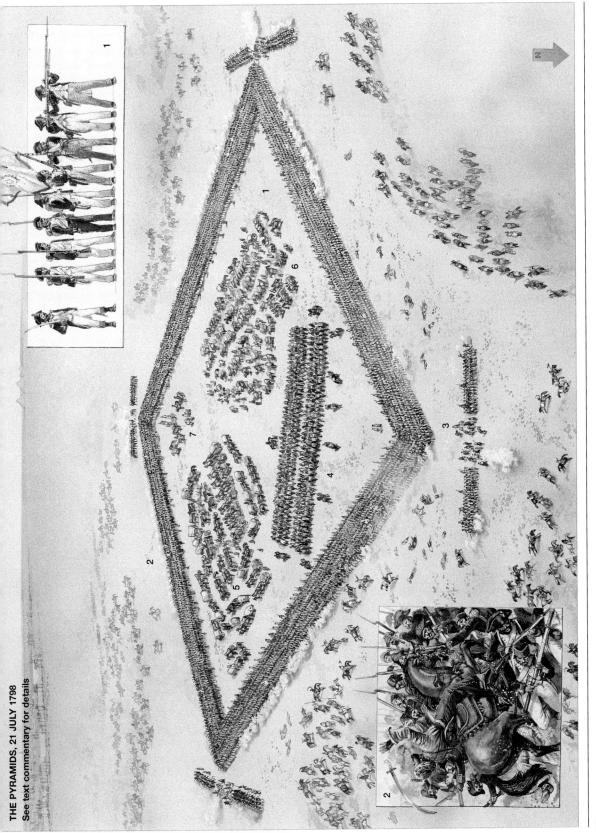

THE PYRAMIDS, 21 JULY 1798
See text commentary for details

C

BERGEN, 19 SEPTEMBER 1799
See text commentary for details

AUERSTADT, 14 OCTOBER 1806
See text commentary for details

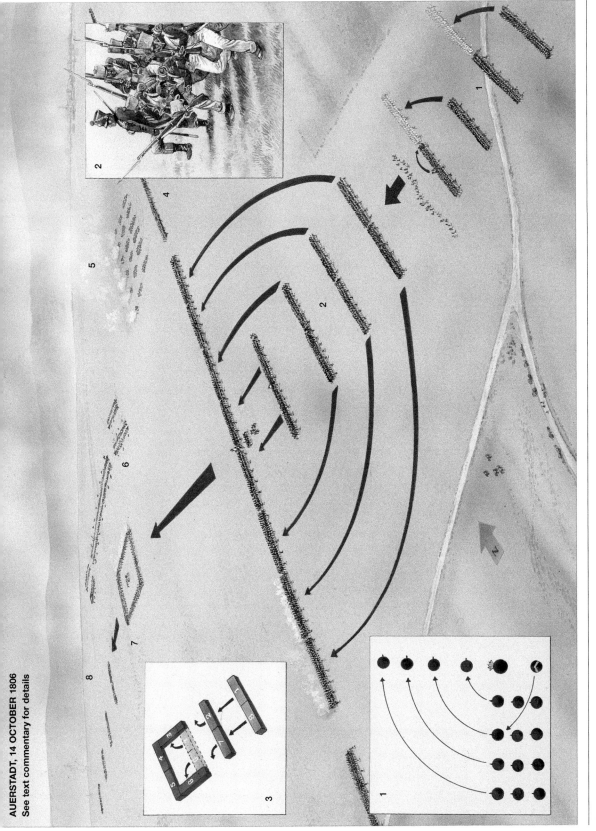

E

F

SORAUREN, 28 JULY 1813
See text commentary for details

G

H

At Austerlitz on 2 December the outnumbered French displayed great tactical virtuosity in both defence and attack. In defence, Marshal Davout lost and then re-took the villages of Telnitz and Sokolnitz in exemplary style, originally using skirmishers ahead of the villages and in the buildings themselves, with artillery and fresh columns in the rear, and exploiting dead ground to conceal the manoeuvres further back. The battle flowed backwards and forwards; but in the end the Austro-Russian attack collapsed. Meanwhile, on the Pratzen heights, Marshal Soult attacked behind a screen of two battalions of skirmishers, with two lines (totalling four regiments) of infantry columns. The first line of these columns would deploy as they came into action – sometimes at a run – and engage the enemy with fire, probably later breaking down into a disorganized skirmish line. They would be counter-attacked from two directions; but their fire, including that of some nine heavy cannon, 'opened great square holes in the enemy lines'.[9] It is noteworthy that these successful defensive victories were achieved by firepower, which is probably a sign that the victorious troops were professionals: it took an amateur to get into a firefight and then lose it.

Firepower and tactical flexibility

Firepower, especially musketry from skirmishers, was also a prominent feature of the Jena campaign of 1806, when the Grande Armée conquered Prussia in short order. In the battles of Saalfeld and Jena itself, the majority of combats seem to have been determined by clouds of

The Pratzen 'heights' at Austerlitz, as seen from the Sokolnitz pheasantry. This photograph shows not only how gentle the slopes could be that led up to 'ground of tactical importance' (contrasting dramatically with the much more genuine 'heights' at Rivoli, Castalla or Bussaco); but also just how open and extensive the battlefield of 2 December 1805 really was. In total it extended 8 miles from end to end, almost all in flat open terrain that could be called a drill-sergeant's paradise – ideal for the formal manoeuvres of large bodies of troops. This is an example of a battlefield on which the terrain posed only negligible obstructions to the evolution of regulation tactics. (Author's collection)

---

[9] Christopher Duffy, *Austerlitz*, p.118, quoting General Thiébault

French skirmishers pouring in their fire over a long period of time. Sometimes whole regiments broke down from formal lines into skirmish order, in a way that was reminiscent of the *grandes bandes* of the early 1790s. However in this case the *débandade* was interspersed by many occasions on which supporting cavalry and artillery were used aggressively and confidently, in a way that had not often been seen in the 1790s. More rigid or 'classic' infantry formations were also employed effectively. As the sun broke through the morning mist, for example, the 34th Regiment was able to make a successful counter-attack with two battalions in line advancing with fire, against a Saxon assault. This represented an untypical moment, since the firefight lasted only a few minutes rather than the protracted affair that was more normal in these battles.

Meanwhile, at Auerstadt on the same day, Gen Morand – 'a reliable but limited officer with a notably small head' (Duffy) – gave a masterclass in tactical virtuosity just south of the village of Hassenhausen (see Plate E). He advanced his Division in columns of march, shook them out into columns of attack, and then into fully deployed lines to give fire; they then formed squares against cavalry, and finally reverted to columns to continue their advance. They were covered all the while by an active skirmish screen, as well as by artillery fire from a flank.

To the present author, it seems that tactical flexibility of this order, unavailable to the armies of the early 1790s, was the hard-earned result of 15 years' combat experience, training and drilling. It was the prize at the end of a learning curve that could not be travelled quickly. To the Prussians of 1806, however, some of these subtleties were not obvious. In their anguished debriefing after Jena they seem to have come to the conclusion that the French fought merely by 'skirmish clouds supported by columns'. There was indeed some truth in this stereotype, and it certainly made for a simple model upon which they could shape their own military renaissance; but there was a lot more to the story than that. Behind the 'skirmish clouds and columns' there were all sorts of other formations that the French could adopt and select at will. The secret of the French success surely lay in the fact that they possessed the cohesion and resilience to adopt whatever tactical arrangements they chose, even in the heat of battle.

In the Polish campaign that followed the same tactical virtuosity was still apparent, although the adverse conditions of terrain and weather blunted some of its sharper edges. This was a winter campaign, in which the Emperor had ordered greatcoats for his army lamentably too late to be of service (in the event they arrived only in May 1807, rather than in January, when they might have been useful). At Eylau on 8 February the battle began before the French were properly concentrated, so they were badly outnumbered for a long time, and suffered especially heavily to Russian artillery, which was twice as numerous as their own. All attempts to fight forward in small columns, monstrous columns, lines or skirmish swarms were doomed to failure, and in falling snow the day ended as an inconclusive but very costly draw. It brought a sudden end to the uninterrupted succession of victories that had begun at Marengo seven years earlier.

The weather had improved by the time of the battle of Friedland on 14 June (the actual anniversary of Marengo), which started with a demonstration by a heavy skirmish screen. Then some of the old tactical virtuosity could again be demonstrated, with a particular emphasis being placed on *l'ordre mixte*. However, there were also some signs that the formations were starting to become excessively heavy. When Gen Marchand made an attack with a massed column of five regiments he was repulsed with heavy losses by the enemy artillery and cavalry. General Bisson then formed up in a long deployed line of nine regiments, but this too was broken by cavalry. Dupont's Division in the rear held out in *ordre mixte,* supported by three of Ney's regiments in square.

After this the tide of battle turned, and the French attacks began to bite. Notable among them was the famous 'artillery charge' by Gen Alexandre-Antoine de Sénarmont, who collected 38 guns from Victor's Corps; he successively advanced them to point-blank range of the enemy infantry – about 60 yards – and riddled it with canister shot. As Gen Foy had once said of artillery tactics, the key thing was to 'get up close and shoot fast'. The Russians were thus eventually routed and thrown back into the River Alle; but it has to be said that the French victory had not been quite as straightforward or as rapid as the Emperor had hoped.

THE PENINSULAR WAR, 1808–14

If conditions in Poland could be harsh, the same was also true in Spain and Portugal, but for different reasons. Mountainous terrain, agricultural shortages and the long distances separating French depots meant that food was always in short supply – the need to gather it could dictate the strategic movements of whole Army Corps. Simultaneously, relentless guerrilla activity made the stretched lines of communication notoriously dangerous and unreliable. Although the French maintained hundreds of thousands of troops in the Peninsula, they were divided up into half a dozen local theatres: Catalonia on the north-east coast; the 'royal road' from Bayonne to Burgos via Vitoria; the remote north-western hills of Galicia; the Portuguese/Spanish frontier region south-west of Salamanca; the central area around Madrid; Andalucia in the south; and, from time to time, Portugal itself.

Thus, instead of one Grande Armée all concentrated for a single offensive thrust, there were usually half a dozen small armies or large Corps, each operating independently under a marshal or senior general. Often these commanders would fail to co-operate with each other, whether for reasons of logistics, manpower shortages, or simple personal jealousies and rivalries. Their operations, moreover, often had the character of static garrison duties or slow-moving sieges rather than of flowing, mobile manoeuvres. On the east coast, for example, it took the French over three years to advance less than 300 miles from Perpignan to finally capture Valencia, which fell only in January 1812.

The French problem was compounded by the fact that many of the troops committed to the Peninsula were 'second line' in quality and experience – and frequently non-French in origin.[10] The Emperor personally visited Spain only once, in 1808–09, and when he withdrew he took his Guard and many other élite troops with him. After that he sent in his military advice from places as far removed as Paris, Vienna

[10] See James Arnold in my *Modern Studies of the War in Spain and Portugal,* Ch 3, 'The French army in the Peninsula'

and Moscow. He also left the Peninsular armies with the now-ageing Gribeauval artillery pieces, while he re-equipped his own favoured Grande Armée with Marmont's new 'Year XI model' guns.

In tactical terms, however, the French usually enjoyed a great advantage. In siege operations, whether in attack or defence, they had the best corps of engineers, and engineer officers, in the world. Only occasionally would their projects run out of control, as happened most famously at Saragossa (20 December 1808 to 20 February 1809). In that epic struggle they did not have to capture a regular fortress that was built and defended according to the well-understood classic rules. Instead, they had to subdue a city's population under arms, who were prepared to defend every block of apartments, room by room, in a war to the knife (or indeed, 'to the bucket of boiling oil'). This type of frenzied house-to-house fighting was not taught in any military school or training camp, and it came as a nasty shock to the infantry who found they had to do it.

Operations against Spanish armies

When it came to battles in the open field, the French won a remarkable series of tactical victories against the Spanish (e.g. at Medina del Rio Seco on 14 July 1808; Tudela, 18 November 1808; Uclés, 13 January 1809; Ocaña, 19 November 1809; and Gebora, 19 February 1811). Even so, they only rarely converted these battlefield victories into conclusive operational successes. In this context we should add that Sir John Moore's defeat in the Coruña campaign of 1809 fitted exactly the same template. His British army was harried and chased all the way through Galicia and then mauled in the final battle, in which he himself was killed; but at least it still managed to slip away to fight another day. On that occasion it got away by sea – an early 19th-century Dunkirk evacuation – whereas many of the Spanish armies that were defeated in battle had been able to escape overland, by putting distance and inhospitable mountain ranges between themselves and their pursuers. At Baílen on 19 July 1808 the Spanish even managed to capture Dupont's French force, which had been sent somewhat rashly into Andalucia to find them.

Baílen aside, the French usually had little difficulty defeating the formed Spanish armies that faced up to them. Importantly, the French cavalry tended to be greatly superior in both quantity and quality to the Spanish cavalry, and this factor was often decisive on the field of battle. The French armies that had fled in panic before Allied cavalry of every nationality, including the Spanish, in 1793–94 were long forgotten. The artillery of the two sides were perhaps somewhat more evenly matched, and the Spanish infantry was often numerically superior. However, it was no longer the manoeuvrable royal army of 1793, but a shakier collection of regular and 'popular' units coming from a variety of different sources. Even the 'second line' French infantry in the Peninsula proved itself capable of seeing off Spanish infantry with some regularity.

View downwards from the summit of the high slope at Bussaco, which Marshal Masséna's army attempted to storm on 27 September 1810. All attempts to use regular formations were completely frustrated by the terrain, as were attempts to deploy from column to line on the summit. A few sharp counter-attacks by Wellington's Anglo-Portuguese army sent the French tumbling back to the valley below. (Author's collection)

As a result of this, when French infantry commanders fought the Spanish they were often tempted to attack in a line of columns without deployment, with musketry provided only by skirmishers. It may be that they had a low opinion of their own soldiers' ability to conduct complex drills in the heat of a battle: this was not the army of the Boulogne camp, after all. Alternatively, the system of undeployed column attacks might be seen as a lazy or careless shortcut – an expression of impatient contempt not only for the enemy, but also for the 'classic' assumption that a firefight in a deployed line should precede any attack. If you could get away with it by staying in column and just pressing on without stopping, shouting *'En avant! Á la baïonette! Vive l'Empereur!'* – then why should you stop to go through all the complicated rigmarole of deploying into line?

Then again, it may be that the idea of attacking in undeployed columns actually reflected a specific ideological position – the revisionist or 'anti-classical' doctrine that the column alone was best in any case. This had been widely discussed since well before the Vaussieux manoeuvres in 1778, and it had been reinforced by a number of combat experiences and tactical writings since 1792. We are surely justified in assuming that at least some of the former Revolutionary generals who ordered these column attacks believed them to be not only the most effective thing to do, but also doctrinally the 'right' thing.

Drum major and band of the 15th Light Infantry, 1807. Apart from drummers in every battalion, each regiment also paid (from its officers' funds) for a splendidly uniformed 'band of music' that included between 16 and 24 wind, brass and percussion instruments, and sometimes a *chapeau chinois* or 'Jingling Johnnie' standard strung with little bells. British officers who fought at Fuentes d'Oñoro recalled watching the French bands play on the open ground between the armies during the lull in the battle on 4 May 1811. However, these musicians tended to be hired-in civilian specialists rather than soldiers; they were notorious for absenting themselves rapidly from any serious fighting, so their tactical significance may be rated as nil. (After Job; Philip Haythornthwaite Collection)

Operations against the British army

Whatever the thought processes that led to undeployed column attacks against the Spanish, they came unstuck when the French came up against the British. These redcoated regulars tended to stand fast in the face of mass attacks. The future Marshal Bugeaud, who had first-hand experience (if from a distance – see below), judged them 'the best infantry in the world – fortunately, there are not many of them'. They were not flustered or panicked by the sheer size of the formations advancing on them, as the Spanish had often been, but instead tended to counter-attack aggressively at close range. French tacticians who failed to distinguish between Spanish and British opponents would therefore tend to be wrong-footed by failing to deploy in sufficient time as they approached a British line, and would find themselves too fully committed inside the danger zone before they finally tried to shake out into line.

Guibert had said that 'any unit which attempts to manoeuvre [i.e. change formation] in front of the enemy is in a state of crisis', and time after time in the Peninsula the French commanders discovered the truth of this adage. A few examples among many may be cited from

Vimeiro in August 1808; Bussaco in September 1810; and Werle's Division at Albuera in May 1811. The same thing would happen again at Waterloo. Indeed, the same tactical misjudgement was even sometimes observed against the Spanish themselves, as at Cardadeu on 16 December 1808 (although there the French columns of the second line then pressed through to win the victory).

To make matters worse, the same commanders rarely faced the British more than once or twice, so they rarely had a chance to progress far along their personal learning curve in this particular respect. British redcoats were a relatively rare breed in the Peninsula as a whole – as in all other theatres – and British forces would often be surrounded and supported by plenty of Allied troops. Thus, at Castalla on 13 April 1813, Suchet's army – which had been fighting in eastern Spain for years against the Spanish alone – on this occasion found that the Spanish had been stiffened by a small force of British. (In fact, this was the only battle against the British that Bugeaud would attend, although in reserve, where he was not a direct participant. He would later famously describe it, although with rather more imagination than his actual proximity to the bayonets justified.) As the French struggled up the steep heights covering Castalla itself, they found they could make no headway against the defenders of the summit. On the southern flank the Spanish were able to make full use of the ground, and after a long struggle repulsed their opponents. Just to their north the two battalions of the French 121st Regiment were sharply counter-attacked by the British 2/27th (Enniskilling) Regiment, which gave a single volley, instantly followed by

A distant view of the ridge at Castalla seen from the west, as it would first have appeared to the French infantry on 13 April 1813. They went on to assault it, but with disastrous consequences. The terrain was too steep and too broken for any regular drill formations to be possible, and the Spanish and British defenders lurking behind the summit enjoyed all the tactical advantages. (Author's collection)

It was not only the British who could fight effectively in defence of hill positions, and we may wonder why the French marshals in the Peninsula did not think more deeply about the example of Rivoli, seen here from the east. This town in northern Italy, sitting on rough high ground, was successfully defended by the French on 14 January 1797. Austrian columns came in from left and right, and from the far side of the town, but all were defeated piecemeal by active French initiatives. It was a triumph of both minor and grand tactics, and was immortalized by the renaming of one of the most prestigious streets in central Paris. (Author's collection)

a bayonet charge. The French were tumbled downhill in short order, with a loss of some 370 men as against 40 British.

It often happened in the Peninsula that the British would select ridgeline positions where they could shelter their main line from view, and from artillery fire from below, until the critical moment arrived when the attacking French were about to reach the summit; then the redcoats would launch inexpensive yet decisive counter-attacks similar to that of the 2/27th at Castalla. From the British point of view this shows an effective tactical use of their normally scarce manpower; and we should add that they sometimes inspired their Portuguese and Spanish allies (e.g. at Bussaco, 1810, and San Marcial, 1813, respectively) to adopt the same system.

From the French point of view, however, it posed a particularly intractable problem. It was simply not possible to conduct all the virtuoso evolutions of the 1791 drill manual when one was climbing a steep slope. Your men would necessarily have to be dispersed, either in skirmish order or in some very ragged version of column or line. Whichever it was, it would be highly vulnerable to a close-range counter-attack by formed troops who were not climbing but charging downhill. The French subaltern Lemonnier-Delafosse complained that at Bussaco the hill was so steep and the footing so difficult that his battalion could not even deploy on a frontage wide enough to form a regulation column of attack. He called the battle an 'escalade without artillery', in which the French had no option but to take the bull by the horns. The French who attacked at Sorauren in 1813 must have had very much the same experience (see Plate G).

'CORRUPT GIGANTISM', 1809–15

We have already noted a number of experiments with heavy columns, not only in the Peninsula but also in the Polish campaign of 1807. These represented a certain falling away from the high standards of flexibility with small units that had been established in 1805, and as the years rolled by thereafter this tendency would become ever more noticeable. After Waterloo the surviving French generals would reflect on the lessons of Bonaparte's whole mad adventure, and many of them would publish their thoughts – most notably Jomini himself, but also Marmont and Morand.[11] The one thing most of them could agree upon was that Bonaparte's biggest mistake had been to indulge in 'corrupt gigantism' during his last six or seven years in power.

By this they meant that when the relatively small but excellent professional army of the Boulogne camp, Austerlitz and Jena had gradually wasted away, it had not been replaced by another cast in the same mould, but by one that was larger but professionally inferior. The Emperor had embraced ever more ambitious commitments, with a corresponding hunger for more cannon-fodder, while suffering from a dilution in the quality of his recruiting pool. In modern terms this is variously called 'overstretch' or 'mission creep'; it seems to be a recurrent phenomenon throughout history when national leaders who have registered a few early successes later develop ever thicker fingers, while looking at ever smaller maps of the world.

Apart from anything else, the battles themselves were getting bigger, or at least those outside the Peninsula. Rightly or wrongly, Bonaparte's enemies perceived that in earlier years the French had often been able to field larger armies than the Austrians and Prussians, because of their use of mass conscription. Now those powers reformed their own military systems in order to catch up. At Marengo the French had deployed 28,000 men against 31,000 Austrians, and at Jena-Auerstadt they had 123,000 against 116,000 Prussians. At Wagram in 1809 the numbers had cranked up to 171,000 against 147,000 Austrians, and it did not stop there. At the battle of Leipzig in 1813 the French would have all of 195,000 men; but the Allies, from all over Europe, were able to put a massive total of 365,000 men into the field. This expansion took place in a relatively short timescale, so there was never enough time for training – especially since the casualties in these battles also continued to grow, including among the experienced NCOs and regimental officers. The half-million men that Bonaparte led into Russia in 1812 were also largely lost to him thereafter. Thus the experience and therefore the quality of the French troops was always falling inexorably away.

Marshal Auguste-Frédéric-Louis Marmont, Duke of Ragusa. One of Bonaparte's leading gunners, he presided over the design of the artillery system of the Year XI. Victorious at Marengo and elsewhere, but defeated at Salamanca, he turned against the Emperor in 1814. He later turned against the Bourbons too, and after the revolution of 1830 he retired to write his memoirs. These contain many retrospective commentaries on infantry tactics, stressing how the 1791 manual should be simplified, and how small battalions were handier than big ones. (After Johnson and Guerin; Philip Haythornthwaite Collection)

11 See my *French Military Thought 1815–51*, Manchester University Press, 1989

Marshal Jacques-Etienne-Joseph-Alexandre Macdonald, Duke of Tarento, was the son of a Scottish Jacobite emigrant. He had served in the royal armies before the Revolution, and then under Dumouriez at Jemappes. He had a chequered career, notably falling out with the Emperor from 1804 to 1807, but he redeemed himself by his attack in a 'monstrous column' at Wagram in 1809 (see Plate F), which earned him promotion to marshal on the field of battle. (Philip Haythornthwaite Collection)

The overcrowded battlefield

In physical terms, the larger numbers of men in a battle were often squeezed into the same space as they had occupied in earlier times. At Waterloo, for example, the main frontage was little more than a mile, which had to accommodate some 250,000 men of all the nationalities engaged. That represented something like 12 times the concentration seen at Austerlitz, where only about 20,000 combatants had fought over each mile of the total frontage of almost 8 miles. It was therefore scarcely surprising if the cramped and crowded late-war battlefields showed more use of massed columns, certainly much bigger than the small and handy battalion columns that had been the norm in 1805–06. The classic case was Macdonald's 'monstrous column' at Wagram (see Plate F), but plenty of other examples have been noted.

One that has often been cited was the attack at Waterloo by D'Erlon's Corps, which was allegedly composed of four Divisions, each in a column of deployed battalions, one behind the other. This obviously made an excessively massed and unwieldy formation, and so it appeared to British observers. (However, from other examples it seems to be a rule that whenever the British reported that they were being attacked by a column of 2,000 men it was actually composed of only 1,000 or even 500 – i.e. the difference between a brigade and a single battalion.) Notwithstanding, it is certainly true that D'Erlon's units turned out to be too closely squashed together one against the other to be able to form battalion squares against cavalry, and they were duly swept away in confusion.

There is more to this episode than simple incompetence on the Corps commander's part, however. Modern research shows that although they never managed to shake out into individual battalions, they did manage to break down into smaller masses than the original monstrous Division columns.[12] Clearly such a move had originally been intended, since an interval of 400m had been left between the Divisions, into which the constituent brigades could deploy. Therefore D'Erlon should not be judged as dismissively as has often been the case – which is the same conclusion that we can reach in the case of Macdonald with his grand *ordre mixte* at Wagram.

We should add that in their attack at the end of the day at Waterloo, some of the French Middle Guard battalion columns did finally deploy into line (see Plate H). This represents a reversion to the 'old' way of doing things, and it shows that the cult of the massed column was not quite as universal as some British authorities have asserted.

The 1808 reforms

Meanwhile the Emperor had been taking a number of measures to try to bolster the combat effectiveness of his infantry. (There were several

---

[12] See John Koontz in *Empires, Eagles and Lions* Nos.78 & 79, March & April 1984

attempts to codify all the various manuals, notably the 1813 *Manuel d'Infanterie ou Resumé de tous les règlements, decrets, usages et renseignements propres aux sous-officiers de cette armée)*.

The first was the Decree of 18 February 1808, which increased the number of men in each platoon from 114 to 140, while reducing each battalion from eight (or technically nine) platoons to six. This had the effect of making each battalion more manoeuvrable but smaller, sometimes to a perilous extent. Especially after less resolute soldiers had fallen out as 'march losses', a battalion that had left its depot with a theoretical strength of 840 might arrive on its eventual battlefield at maybe half that strength, or still less (if it had been badly recruited in the first place, and especially if it had already fought the enemy somewhere along the way). In the 1814 campaign, when all these considerations applied, it was not unusual to find battalions going into action with just 200 men. However, it is worth noticing that the proportion of officers, NCOs and old soldiers who fell out as 'march losses' was always much lower than that among the raw young conscripts. Paradoxically, this meant that the more men fell out, the higher the average quality of the ones who were left.

This print is entitled 'mutual instruction'; the Old Guard veteran firing his musket is instructing his younger comrade in the manual of arms. This reflects the established French practice of 'surveillance', whereby older soldiers were supposed to look after greenhorns. The Young Guard soldier is reaching into his pouch for the next cartridge – the 3rd movement of the loading drill, following the opening of the flintlock action by pulling the hammer back to half-cock position. (After Charlet; Philip Haythornthwaite Collection)

A line of young, inexperienced but enthusiastic 'Marie Louises' of the 1814 campaign in northern France, reassuring their Emperor that he can rely upon them 'as if they were the Old Guard'. The complete 1812 pattern uniforms shown here are as unrealistic as that boast – most would have been lucky to get a greatcoat and a forage cap. Like the Volkssturm teenagers who were sacrificed for Hitler in 1945, these green draftees would quickly be mown down in huge numbers. (After Raffet; Philip Haythornthwaite Collection)

The reorganization of 1808 also increased the proportion of theoretically 'élite' troops (grenadiers and voltigeurs) from one in nine to one in three. This regularized the provision of supposed élites within each battalion, where previously the arrangements had been very variable and even haphazard. This may not have done much to improve the basic quality of the new recruits, but it did at least demonstrate an intention to give formal recognition and status to the more experienced soldiers. It had always been a key principle in the French army that the older soldiers should watch over *(surveiller)* the younger ones, and bring them forward by setting them an example of military virtues. Bonaparte had already demonstrated this on a bigger scale by according generous privileges to his veteran *grognards* when they were accepted into his Imperial Guard.

Another measure that Bonaparte took to stiffen his infantry was to increase the ratio of artillery that supported it. He reasoned that the morale of shaky troops could be bolstered if they saw large masses of guns firing on their behalf, almost irrespective of the effect on the enemy. There were two elements in this reform. The first was that he provided more guns per man: whereas in 1805–06 the figure had been slightly less than 2 guns per thousand troops, in 1807–09 it was well over 2 guns, and for the 1812 campaign it reached an average of 3.5 pieces. On the battlefield of Borodino there were in fact almost 5 guns per thousand French soldiers, although that was still less than the Russian ratio. In the period 1809–12 Bonaparte even returned to the use of 'battalion guns' – notionally two light pieces per battalion – which had been abandoned in 1796 as too cumbersome.

Secondly, the art of making rapid artillery concentrations at key points was perfected. In part this was due to an increasing proportion of horse artillery, which could be directed quickly from a central reserve to threatened parts of the battlefield. It was also in part a reflection of the growing size of the artillery of the Imperial Guard, which could be used in battle as an 'army level' reserve of firepower. At both Wagram (1809) and Borodino (1812) *grandes batteries* of over 100 guns would be massed at the height of the battle, and towards the end of the battle of Lützen (1813) an 'artillery charge' with 60 guns was locally decisive.

* * *

Overall, therefore, we can say that the size and shape of battles changed quite significantly between Austerlitz and Waterloo, in a way that it had not done between Valmy and Marengo. The tactics became less refined, if such a term can ever be used in this brutal context. The generals continued to be well versed in the *Règlement* of 1791, but in practice they increasingly simplified it. In part this was because it needed to be simplified, as had been widely debated at Boulogne; but in part

Two members of the Young Guard firing at will. Although they appear to be part of a formed line they seem to have 'paired off' in the manner recommended for skirmishers, one firing while the other reloads. (After Raffet; Philip Haythornthwaite Collection)

it was also a recognition that the more recent drafts could not execute the complex manoeuvres that had been seen in the Grande Armée at its height.

In the years after Waterloo there would be an attempt to return to the 1805 way of doing things, and the idea of a 'small but good' army persisted until it was finally defeated in 1870. Even when the *Règlement* was revised in the 1830s it was not changed in any very radical way, and its influence lived on. In fact, we can see it as a robust and versatile system for manoeuvres that could be adapted to the needs of any type of army, whether big or small in size or good or bad in quality.

FURTHER READING

Only a tiny fraction of the books consulted can be mentioned here, and then only works in English:

James Arnold, 'Column versus line in the Napoleonic Wars. A reappraisal' in *Journal of the Society for Army Historical Research*, LX (1983), pp.196–208

David G.Chandler, *The Campaigns of Napoleon* (Weidenfeld & Nicolson, London 1967)

Christopher Duffy, *Austerlitz 1805* (Seeley Service, London 1977)

Empires, Eagles and Lions magazine, 1st series 1976–92 (first published by the New Jersey Association of Wargamers, then, from issue 62, by the RAFM Company, Ontario, Canada). A splendid forum for detailed tactical discussion.

Paddy Griffith, *The Art of War of Revolutionary France, 1789–1802* (Greenhill, London 1998)

Paddy Griffith (ed), *Modern studies of the war in Spain and Portugal, 1808–14* (Volume 9 of Sir Charles Oman's *History of the Peninsular War;* Greenhill, London 1999). For tactics note especially Chs 3, 10 & 11, by James Arnold, Arthur Harman and Brent Nosworthy respectively.

Patrick Griffith, *French Artillery 1800–15* (Almark, London 1976)

B.P.Hughes, *Firepower – Weapons effectiveness on the battlefield, 1630–1850* (Arms & Armour Press, London 1974)

John Lynn, *Bayonets of the Republic – Motivation and tactics in the army of Revolutionary France* (University of Illinois Press, 1984)

George Nafziger, *Imperial Bayonets* (Greenhill, London 1996)

The Napoleon Series at http://www.napoleon-series.org. An exceptionally well-informed discussion group.

Brent Nosworthy, *Battle Tactics of Napoleon and his Enemies* (Constable edn, London 1995)

Charles Oman, 'Line and Column in the Peninsula War' (first published in *Proceedings of the British Academy,* Vol 4, London 1910; reprinted in *Wellington's Army,* London 1912). This article memorably, if misleadingly, called attention to the issues involved. See discussions in James Arnold's articles cited above, and in my *Forward into Battle* (1981; 2nd edn, Crowood Press, Ramsbury, UK, 1990), Chs 2 & 3.

R.S.Quimby, *The Background of Napoleonic Warfare* (Columbia University Press, 1957). Essentially a translation of the works of Cdt J.Colin.

PLATE COMMENTARIES

A: JEMAPPES, 6 NOVEMBER 1792:
Skirmishers, 'blobs' and 'swarms'

Jemappes, on the outskirts of Mons, was the first major offensive battle fought by the freshly raised army of the young Revolutionary regime. General Dumouriez successfully brought an overwhelming numerical superiority into the field, with some 40,000 French troops against just 13,000 Austrians. He also successfully formed up his men in textbook manner, with skirmishers in front, then a line of battalions deployed into line, followed by lines of reserve battalions in various kinds of column. A five-hour preliminary bombardment began at 7am, which pushed back the Austrian front line from the base of a low rise to its crest, which was strengthened by a series of redoubts.

At noon a general attack was launched all along the front, and the plate depicts a section of the fighting about half an hour after combat had been joined. We see the left flank of Dumouriez's central assault, near the village of Quaregnon (not shown – a few hundred yards to the left rear of the French flank). The French advanced across meadows to storm the lightly wooded slope, at the top of which the Austrians had established a strong line supported by reserves. About a mile to the north, the spire of the church in Jemappes village can be seen; off the picture to the right would be the remainder of the main assault, as well as several lesser attacks on the Austrian east flank around the village of Cuesmes.

In later patriotic literature it was often assumed that Dumouriez had formed up three or four very large columns (of which his central assault presumably formed the largest), which simply charged forward *en masse* and drove off the Austrians by force of revolutionary fervour. In reality, each battalion attacked separately, was initially checked, and often fell into disarray; it would take several hours of confused fighting before the Austrians finally withdrew. At Jemappes, French battalions averaged about 500 men.

At (**1**) battle smoke rises over Jemappes village, as a French diversionary attack on this extreme north flank of the Austrian position is held at bay.

Guns in the Austrian redoubts (**2**) fire on the French advance; while providing protection for artillery the redoubts also make excellent targets, and will eventually be silenced by French guns. The original Austrian front line (**3**), which started the day at the foot of the slope, has been forced back to the top, and has performed a 'passage of lines' by retreating through spaces opened in the second line waiting on the crest. The original second line has thus become the front line and, after closing up its spacing, is giving musketry fire from a continuous line; meanwhile the original front-line units have reformed as the new second line. Along the slopes below the crest, French and Austrian skirmishers exchange fire (**4**). The French are more numerous, and are being reinforced in a confused and unplanned way by over-eager individuals coming forwards from the battalions to their rear. At (**5**), a 'regular' battalion – composed of remnants of an old royal regiment, reinforced with recent drafts – has failed to deploy successfully from column into line under fire. It is on the point of falling into a shapeless mass, in which some men are firing,

some running forward to join the skirmish line, and others doing nothing – or thinking about sneaking away to the rear. It will have to be reinforced or replaced with a fresh battalion coming up from the second line. On its right at (**6**), a 'national' battalion – newly raised from volunteers – has successfully deployed from the column (**7**) in which it approached, into a three-deep line to give fire. As the battle continues it will rapidly lose its regulation dressing and become a somewhat ragged 'swarm' of musketeers, but it will continue to develop fire. It is not necessarily true that 'national' units all suffered from poor discipline and morale, and in the early days of the Revolutionary Wars they were often the best troops available. However, in the icy winter of 1792/93 many of those who had initially volunteered enthusiastically to defend France would choose to absent themselves from garrison duties in Belgium with equal enthusiasm. New methods then had to be developed to fill the gaps in the ranks, but the most important of these – conscription – proved very unpopular among the civilian population.

(**Inset 1**) shows a file of infantry giving fire. It had been found impractical for third-rank men to fire effectively (and safely) past the two men in front of them, so the third man was expected to reload muskets that they passed back to him. In practice this did not work either: nobody wanted to hand his personal weapon over to someone else in the heat of combat. Consequently the third rank often did not really participate in the firefight, unless they were detached (or detached themselves) to join the skirmishers. In any case, there were never enough muskets to go round, and the third rank was sometimes equipped with pikes.

(**Inset 2**) shows infantry skirmishing in scrubby woodland. The correct method was for pairs of men to act together, one reloading while the second was ready to fire, so that one of them would always have a loaded weapon ready to meet any emergency.

B: WATTIGNIES, 15 OCTOBER 1793:
Weakness against in-depth defences

This depicts a scene at about 2pm on the first day of the battle, when the French made no progress – although they would be victorious the following day. Brigade General Antoine Balland's 13,000-strong Division is attacking the Austrians in the area of the village of Dourlers, about half way between Avesnes and Mauberge. This was the central of three attacks, spaced about 3¾ miles apart, that were launched simultaneously by Gen Jourdan, commanding the joint armies of 'the North' and 'the Ardennes'; the attack on Wattignies itself (today, Wattignies la Victoire) was taking place nearly 4 miles to the north-east. The politician Carnot – an academically minded captain of engineers – happened to be 'on mission' at the time, visiting Jourdan's army on behalf of the Committee of Public Safety. He insisted that the assault should be started prematurely, so it suffered some avoidable disorganization. This was far from a unique example of direct political interference in tactical decisions during 1793–94.

Balland began in fine style, advancing northwards downhill from the village of Trois Pavés, across a stream defended by Austrian outposts (not shown – off the right-hand side of the illustration), and then up towards the crest of another ridge. This screened Dourlers, which nestled in the valley of a stream some 600–700 yards to the north, thus protected from long-range French artillery fire. The leading French infantry quickly cleared the ridge, only to come under fire from Austrian cannon ranged along a second ridge north of and about 1,100 yards beyond the village (not shown – off the left-hand side of the illustration). This bombardment not only hit the infantry, but also smashed a battery of their horse artillery as it attempted to deploy among them. Thus the French found themselves exposed to heavy fire on a forward slope, and without any artillery of their own.

Less than 200 yards ahead of them the sunken De Monceau lane ran across the slope, manned by Bohemian grenadiers firing from covered positions along its southern edge. Beyond these, the houses, church and château of Dourlers had been barricaded and occupied by more Austrian troops – and beyond these, and their supporting batteries on the second ridge behind, the main Austrian line still lay far out of reach on yet a third, more northerly ridge. At Wattignies the French discovered the difficulty of tackling a defence in depth, especially without proper artillery support.

After the loss of their horse battery they eventually brought up heavy guns from Trois Pavés, but these were never enough. The infantry had to make three attacks before they finally managed to clear the Bohemians out of the sunken lane, at the cost not only of casualties but also of much

disruption. By the time Balland was able to rally his troops to assault the village they were already partly disorganized, and they failed to capture it at the first onset. The illustration shows the point at which the battle began to degenerate into protracted and scrappy skirmishing, with perhaps 8,000 French being held at bay by some 3,000 Austrians.

After a considerable time Dourlers did finally fall, and the French – now in a formless mass – managed to advance over the second rise beyond and down into the valley of the Bracquinière stream, just below the Austrian main positions. Upon arrival there they were sitting ducks; they suffered close-range artillery fire and then a cavalry attack on their flank, which sent them pell mell back to their starting position at Trois Pavés.

The average starting strength of the eight battalions in Balland's Division had been 582 men each. The crest line (1) that they initially captured shows the wreckage of the horse artillery battery (2) destroyed by Austrian guns as it arrived on the ridge. Capturing the sunken lane (3) has cost heavy casualties, and has left Balland's battalion columns of attack (4) disorganized as they continued to advance under Austrian artillery fire down the slopes towards Dourlers. The standard method of preparing a village for defence was to barricade the streets and fortify as many houses as possible, particularly exploiting the strength of any larger, stone-built structures – in this case, the church and the château (5). French foot artillery (6) arrives belatedly from Trois Pavés to support the assault on the village; it lacked the mobility to keep up with infantry and cavalry advancing across country, and often arrived late.

(Inset 1) The colour party of each battalion marched at the centre with the flag in the front rank, acting as an essential marker to show the unit's current location, intended direction and pace. It helped the men of the battalion to keep alignment, and higher commanders to keep track of the unit. The party was supposed to consist of six corporals, two sergeants, and a sergeant-major colour-bearer – in theory, the best NCOs available from all the platoons of the battalion. Those reconstructed here are largely dressed in regulation 1791 uniforms for the 49e de Ligne – a unit of Balland's Division; we have chosen to show the two sergeants flanking the colour-bearer sporting the bearskins and epaulettes of grenadiers.

(Inset 2) Horse or light artillery was one of the great innovations of the Revolutionary army, considered to be a new arm, separate from the artillery proper. Created in 1792 to provide close co-operation in fast-moving operations, it exploited its far superior mobility to that of foot artillery. All 84 men of each battery were mounted, and 8-pdr Gribeauval guns and caissons had six-horse teams instead of the usual

A grenadier drummer in the 1790s who is also a fifer. The fifes could lighten the mood of troops on the march, but in battle it was the drums alone that could be heard. The importance of drums in battle was to re-broadcast tactical instructions from the battalion commander to the troops, in a manner that would be audible above the din of gunfire. The ominous drum roll for ordering the 'charge' was rendered by the French as the rhythm 'PLAN rat a PLAN rat a PLAN (etc)', which British witnesses famously remembered as 'OLD trousers, OLD trousers, OLD trousers (etc)'. (After Orange; Philip Haythornthwaite Collection)

four. In time horse gunners would also come to adopt some of the fancy uniform distinctions and panache of the cavalry, and enemy venturing too close were as likely to face a sabre charge as grapeshot. This sense of élite status would survive incorporation into the main artillery arm in 1795.

C: THE PYRAMIDS, 21 JULY 1798:
An 'Egyptian square' in action

Many artists have portrayed the battle as if it were fought only a few hundred yards from the Pyramids of Giza themselves, but in fact it is doubtful that the combatants could even see them – certainly not once battle was joined, and the air was filled with powder-smoke and the dust raised by thousands of horses. They were about ten miles distant to the south (top centre); the city of Cairo (top left) was perhaps half that distance away to the south-east, over on the eastern bank of the Nile. The intervening ground was flat and gently undulating sand – so flat, indeed, that today it is the site of an international airport.

The main threat to the French was the strong Mameluke force of élite light cavalry – often high-born, but essentially 'irregular' in European terms – rather than their unmanoeuvrable infantry or artillery. Bonaparte therefore formed his army into five giant marching squares, each a Division strong, to provide all-round defence. Unlike the three ranks of a conventional battalion square, the sides of these large formations were eight ranks deep. The four corners were strengthened with pairs of cannon and detached grenadier platoons, while the interior sheltered the cavalry, artillery vehicles, baggage train and staff. The infantry opened fire at about 50 paces, laying down a wall of lead that held off the milling masses of Mameluke horsemen; only a few determined individuals managed to get close enough to use their scimitars, pistols and blunderbusses, and French casualties were few. As one of the defenders reported: 'The number of corpses surrounding our square was soon considerable, and the clothes of the dead and wounded Mamelukes were burning like tinder... The blazing wads from our muskets penetrated at the same time as our bullets through their rich uniforms, which were embroidered with gold and silver and floated as lightly as gauze.'

We reconstruct here the square formed by the 5,000-odd men of the Division of Gen Louis Desaix, which led the southward advance (**1**). The leading corner of the square points in the direction of march, making it in effect a 'diamond'. Arranging the squares facing corner-to-corner, rather than with the faces opposite one another, ensures that when any face of a square opens fire its bullets will be angled away from adjoining squares that might be on the same line. Desaix's square consists of three *demi-brigades de bataille* – the 21e Légère, 61e de Ligne and 88e de Ligne – each of them three battalions strong. The average strength of these nine battalions is about 500 men, giving some 1,125 in each side of the square, in eight ranks and 125 files (**2**). The flags of each demi-brigade and each battalion mark its position; the 21e Légère formed this south-eastern face, the 61e de Ligne the north-eastern face (left) and half the north-western, and the 88e the right-hand half of the north-western and the whole of the south-western (right) face. In such a closed and non-regulation formation, however, the men of different battalions must have become somewhat mixed up; it is not clear just how the normal three-rank lines were divided up to

make a total of eight, and drill-sergeants trying to maintain orderly ranks and files must have faced great difficulties. (At this date the new locally made coloured uniforms and 'pouffe' caps had not yet been issued, so most units would have looked alike.)

Outside each corner is a section of two guns (**3**), each of which fires only when the other has reloaded, so that there is always a reserve of fire. Each pair of guns is protected by two platoons of grenadiers detached from their battalions. Inside the square the Division's attached cavalry – the 7e*bis* Régiment de Hussards (**4**) – are sheltering, ready to charge out if necessary. Ahead of them are the artillery vehicles (**5**) on one side, and a mass of baggage animals, carts and their drivers (**6**) on the other. Inside the leading angle are Gen Desaix and his staff (**7**). All elements had to be ready to move at the same pace as the infantry, and the square could only move very slowly without losing its solidity.

(**Inset 1**) Cross-section of a file in an 'Egyptian square', including a colour-bearer. Only the front two ranks can fire their muskets or level their bayonets, while the ranks behind must keep their weapons safely shouldered. The flag must be displayed as near to the front rank as possible, but in this formation it is thought prudent to give it the protection of two fighting ranks. The 'ninth rank', a pace behind the eighth, is made up of the platoon's subaltern officers and some of its sergeants, who act as file-closers.

(**Inset 2**) Normally the combination of firepower and a wall of levelled bayonets would be enough to keep the enemy's horses at a respectful distance, but occasionally one might get through. If a horse was brought down just as it was charging into the front rank it could crush some infantrymen and knock over many more, creating ripples of disruption in all directions. This could be a very dangerous moment, especially if other cavalrymen were at hand to exploit the breach. In Europe squares were sometimes completely broken as a result of such incidents, although this did not happen at the battle of the Pyramids.

D: BERGEN, 19 SEPTEMBER 1799:
Defence and recapture of a village

After the French had failed to destroy the Duke of York's expedition to north Holland the latter was reinforced by a strong if inexperienced force of Russian infantry. This enabled the Allies to switch to the offensive in the direction of Alkmaar, the first phase including an attack on the village of Bergen. Some 7,000 Russians moved off at 3.30am, although the darkness did not help them maintain the orderly dressing of their ranks. Dawn exposed them marching south down an open beach, and they came under a galling fire from French skirmishers in the sand dunes; disorder spread, and some Russian columns even fired into one another in the confusion. Nevertheless, their enthusiasm carried them forward, and they were able to capture the village by about 8am. The French had received very little warning of this attack, and a strong wind from the south-west carried away the first sounds of firing; General of Brigade Louis-Jean-Baptiste Gouvion was therefore forced to set up his defences very hastily. His 42e Demi-Brigade, some 2,000 strong with five guns in support, fought stubbornly – at first along the northern edge of the houses, and then falling back through them and out the southern side of the village. The principles of 'defence in depth' (which had served the

57

Austrians so well at Dourlers – Plate B) should then have provided an immediate counter-attack by heavy columns held in rear of the village. At Bergen, however, there were no such supports immediately to hand, and it took some frantic staffwork to call some in from a distance.

The illustration shows the counter-attack by the 4e Demi-Brigade going in at about 10am. This cleared out the weary and ill co-ordinated Russians in house-to-house fighting at the point of the bayonet. Subsequently a stream of Russian fugitives emerged from the far side of the village – and it was then that the French played their trump card, in the form of cavalry wheeling around the inland flank to hit the rear of the village and disperse the Russians before they could rally. Meanwhile a column of French troops hooked round far to the east, behind the scene of the fighting, to block any retreat; several thousand Russians were captured. The remnants of the Allied army then retired hastily to their starting positions; and Gouvion was promoted general of division that evening.

The remainder of the campaign saw renewed Allied attacks on 2 and 6 October. The first outflanked and captured both Bergen and Alkmaar after confused fighting; but the second ran into a well-organized French 'mobile defence in depth' at the village of Kastricum south of Bergen. There the Russians suffered a defeat that was almost a carbon-copy of that on 19 September; this time, however, the Allies continued retreating all the way to their ships.

The village of Bergen (1) includes strongpoints in the mill and the brick-built manor house, as well as less easily defended smaller buildings of brick or timber. The survivors of the 42e Demi-Brigade (2) are seen falling back after being driven from the village, while two battalions of the 4e Demi-Brigade (3) advance to the counter-attack in columns of division; average battalion strength was 617 men. Two squadrons of French cavalry (4) are about to advance to encircle the village and catch fugitives from its northern and eastern sides – an extremely effective tactic, in close support of the main infantry attack. Each squadron is drawn up in two ranks, on a frontage of about 75 riders – thus roughly three times the width of the two-platoon infantry divisions. Meanwhile, inland to the east, another French force (5) hooks wide around the battlefield to cut the Russians off from the rear. This demonstrates co-ordination and foresight of a high order in the planning of the French mobile defence.

(Inset 1) Regular drills and manoeuvres were impossible in house-to-house fighting in built-up areas, such as took place in Bergen. Troops could either be dispersed to defend individual doorways, windows, and loopholes pickaxed through the brickwork; or massed to hold barricades or charge in columns down streets and into courtyards. Commanders knew that in these circumstances numbers were less important than determination, and relatively few defenders might hope to disrupt and delay even the heaviest attacks.

(Inset 2) 'Sacrificial leadership'. In theory the drill manual called for officers and NCOs to position themselves either on the flanks of their platoons or behind them (with the single exception of the battalion adjutant-major in an advance, when he was to ride 40 paces ahead of the flag to give it direction). In practice, however, officers saw it as their duty to encourage their men by example, so if the troops hesitated then their leaders would move ahead of them and

exhort them to follow. French officers often displayed these qualities in action, however aloof they might hold themselves at other times. British observers of battles in the Peninsula often noted that it led to undue officer casualties.

E: AUERSTADT, 14 OCTOBER 1806: Morand's flexible manoeuvres

In this phase of the decisive battle of Jena-Auerstadt, the heavily outnumbered French were attacked by the Prussian main body under the Duke of Brunswick; but Marshal Louis-Nicolas Davout stopped them in their tracks with his III Corps around Hassenhausen. Davout deployed two Divisions in and to the north-west of that village (top right), absorbing the initial Prussian onslaught – during which, incidentally, the Duke of Brunswick was mortally wounded. General Charles Morand's 1st Division was then sent to occupy a west-facing frontage of about 1¼ miles to the open south-eastern side of Hassenhausen. Morand had some 9,000 men in nine battalions, 12 guns (which he massed to the right of his infantry), and 'some cavalry'. Here we reconstruct in semi-diagrammatic form the movements of the third battalion of Morand's force to arrive on the battlefield – the 1er Bataillon of the 61e Régiment de Ligne. It provides an excellent example of the French infantry's ability by 1805–06 to conduct the full range of drill-book manoeuvres under fire.

At the start of the day Morand's men hastened to the battlefield along the road already followed by the previous two Divisions of III Corps. The formation was initially a column of platoons (which might have to be doubled down to half-platoons at particularly narrow points), with two battalions of the 13e Léger in the lead to act as a screen and a flank guard around Hassenhausen. Next came the two battalions of the 61e de Ligne, followed by two of the 51e, two of the 20e, and one of the 17e de Ligne.

When approaching its designated fighting ground left of the 13e Léger the 1/61e veered off the road, allowing the battalions that followed it to fan out and take up positions successively further to its left. Each battalion deployed from column of platoons into column of divisions while still on the march, putting out a screen of skirmishers ahead; and then, upon arrival in position, into a fully deployed line three ranks deep, ready to deliver musketry. Morand's assigned frontage was so wide that his Division was necessarily drawn up in a single line of battalions, rather than the more normal two lines that could provide an insurance against local enemy breakthroughs.

Morand's men deployed successfully in the nick of time, and did not buckle when some of Gen Wartensleben's infantry attacked them (not illustrated). After a firefight the Prussians retreated; Morand's Division had plugged a wide gap to the south of Davout's position, and beaten off the threat. However, the retreat of the Prussian infantry allowed a new attack from the north by Blücher's cavalry. Morand's order for his units to form battalion squares was executed as calmly as the earlier transition from column to line. The Prussian horse were seen off, after which Davout correctly judged that the enemy's impetus was exhausted and his troops disorganized. He ordered a general advance, and Morand's Division changed from a line of battalion squares to a line of battalion columns of attack. This movement was entirely successful, and the Prussians were driven from the battlefield. While Morand was hit in the arm by a canister-ball, he could congratulate himself that his Division's performance had helped achieve a major victory against double his own numbers. This battle has justly been acclaimed as a masterpiece of tactical virtuosity, demonstrating the high quality of the Grande Armée at its peak of maturity.

The illustration shows successive stages. At (**1**), the 1/61e deploys from column of march (column of platoons or half-platoons) into column of attack (column of divisions), each second platoon moving up on the flank of the platoon ahead of it. A skirmish screen is also thrown forward; this will extend the southern flank of those from the 13e Léger already skirmishing further to the right around Hassenhausen village. As the battalion – with an average strength of about 750 men – advances to its designated fighting line, it deploys on its lead division from column of attack into a three-deep line. This is achieved by Guibert's innovative method as incorporated in the 1791 drill manual: the lead division becomes the centre of

the line, and each of the three following divisions splits into its two component platoons, which move out and forward to take position on either side of those ahead (**2**). Attacked by Prussian infantry, the newly formed line of the 1/61e gives fire by platoons (**3**), with its right flank secured by the 13e Léger (**4**) and the Division's artillery (**5**).

When the Prussian infantry fall back it is the turn of Blücher's cavalry (**6**). Each battalion forms square (**7**), in a 'diamond' arangement to avoid friendly fire. For a time each square is surrounded by Prussian horsemen, but they fail to break them and retire to regroup. When Davout orders a general advance, Morand's battalions change back from square into columns of attack (**8**), and help drive the enemy off the field.

(**Inset 1**) The theory. The difficulty for all troops when changing formation was that during the movement itself they were not in any easily recognizable order, but in a transitional state between one clear layout and the next. This diagram shows a detail of a drill-book provision for wheeling a three-deep platoon from facing the front to facing the right flank. The captain, at the extreme right of the front rank, stands fast and turns through 90°. But each file to his left has to march successively further and faster before they are in position; the file on the extreme left might have to cover as much as 30 yards before reaching its correct new place. Each file

The last 11 movements of the 18-movement sequence for loading the musket, shown in the French manual of arms – from 'Cartouche dans le canon' at top left, to 'En joue' at bottom right. In the captions an '=' sign shows the pause between the 'preparatory' and 'executive' words of command. (Anne S.K.Browne Library, Providence, RI)

would have to follow a circling path, so both direction and alignment would have to change with each pace – and each file would ideally be marching at a different speed from its neighbours. Meanwhile the sergeant, who had been behind the captain on the right flank of the third rank, had to move to take up the same position in the new layout.

(**Inset 2**) The practice. There was plentiful opportunity for confusion during even the simplest change of formation, by the best-trained troops. The men might not hear an order clearly, or might misunderstand what they were meant to do. Uneven ground could delay some while others raced ahead, and casualties might disrupt the movement. If the enemy – and worst of all, a cavalry attack – managed to hit a unit while it was between formations, the results could be devastating.

(**Inset 3**) There were many ways to form a battalion square, depending upon the starting formation. Here, platoons wheel outwards from column of divisions.

F: WAGRAM, 6 JULY 1809:
Macdonald's 'monstrous column'

At a climax of the battle of Wagram a dangerous gap appeared in the French line, between the villages of Süssenbrun and Aderklaa. To fill it, Bonaparte called up Gen Etienne Macdonald's Corps of the Army of Italy consisting of the Divisions of Gens Lamarque and Broussier, totalling 21 battalions. However, this force had suffered a panic rout only 18 hours earlier; it had not fully recovered either its morale or its stragglers, and its strength was only some 6,000 men. The Corps was supported by cavalry, and by a massed battery of over 100 guns already deployed on its right flank, towards Aderklaa. The first threat that Macdonald faced in his advance across the level battlefield was from Austrian cavalry; so he formed his weak Corps into a sort of gigantic square, reminiscent in some ways of those seen in Egypt

It takes time and expert instruction to master the skills of military choreography, and the art of close-order drill (see Plate E insets) survive today only for ceremonial. Here officer cadets at the British Royal Military Academy, Sandhurst, practise during the 1970s; to the drill-masters of the 1791 French *Règlement* they would appear ridiculously widely dispersed. They are not maintaining 'touch of elbows' between each man in the same rank, and the second rank is following the first at two full paces rather than the 13in demanded by the drill book. (Author's collection)

(Plate C), although in this case the rear was filled by supporting cavalry. This feature, and the fact that he would later mount an attack with it, has led commentators to refer to the formation as a variant of the *ordre mixte* or, more often, as 'Macdonald's monstrous column'. As such it has achieved a certain notoriety in the annals of Napoleonic tactics.

No two historians agree on the exact formation used, but most believe that the front face was a line of eight battalions in columns at close distance, so the overall frontage may have been no more than about 380 yards. Behind each flank was a column of battalions drawn up in column, but the numbers are variously quoted; here we assume four battalions on the left and nine on the right. However many there were, they and their supporting arms seem to have been steady enough to beat off Austrian cavalry before moving on to the offensive. The whole unwieldy mass advanced against the Austrian infantry around Süssenbrun, where it ground to a halt at about 1pm and engaged in a protracted firefight – as shown at the top of this illustration.

Eventually this deadlock was broken by the arrival of reinforcements – the remainder of the Army of Italy and

Wrede's Saxons; between them, they all managed to capture Süssenbrun by about 3pm, cementing French victory in the battle as a whole. As a result, Macdonald was promoted marshal on the battlefield – the only one of Bonaparte's officers who would be so honoured.

Macdonald's 'column' (**1**) might equally be called a 'square' or even an '*ordre mixte*'. The infantry battalions have an average strength of a mere 286 men – about 30 per cent of the official establishment of 940, and giving each division a frontage of only about 32 men. All units are using close spacing, not only between their three divisions but between one battalion and the next. Despite the large open space in the middle of the formation, therefore, its constituent troops must be seen as 'massed'. Note that 'battalion guns' are positioned in the intervals between at least the leading battalions. Their caissons, and the Corps and Division staffs (**2**), remain in close touch with the infantry protecting them. Three cavalry regiments (**3**) wait in the rear, ready to exploit counter-attacks once the enemy cavalry (**4**) have been beaten off by the infantry. Macdonald's right flank is protected by a grand battery of over 100 guns – its left end just visible at (**5**) – including the reserve artillery of the Imperial Guard. Although something similar had often been seen in earlier battles, it had rarely been on this grandiose scale. However, in the gigantic battles of 1812–13 in Russia and Saxony such huge artillery concentrations would become increasingly commonplace, on both sides. The battlefield (**6**) was known as the *Marchfeld* or 'Parade Ground', its flat open fields providing an ideal site for the Vienna garrison's annual manoeuvres after the autumn harvest. However, in July 1809 the corn had not yet been cut; dry under the hot summer sun, it was ignited in some places by the burning wads fired from the guns, and wounded men who were caught in the blaze died horribly.

In the top part of the illustration (**7**), Macdonald's men approach the Austrian strongpoint of Süssenbrun, suffering increasing casualties the closer they approach and the further they move from their own supporting artillery. Eventually the weakened line stops in some confusion. An attempt is made to outflank the village from the north – Macdonald's right – but this too is stalled.

(**Inset 1**) Macdonald's column would become known not only for its dense massing, but also for the large numbers of men who fell out during its advance. Allegedly only a fairly small proportion were actually hit, but many more pretended to be, or 'helped the wounded to the rear' – or were simply skulkers who deserted the ranks and robbed their fallen comrades. Accounts vary as to whether it was 19 per cent or only 9 per cent of the starting strength that eventually remained standing by the end of the battle; but there was a general feeling that the heavier the column that started off for an attack, the greater would be the proportion of stragglers.

(**Inset 2**) At Aspern-Essling in May 1809 it had been realized that the high training standards of the Boulogne camp had been diluted, by new drafts and by the demands of 'strategic overstretch' – i.e. the detachment of forces for Spain. In order to boost the sagging quality of his infantry, Bonaparte re-introduced 'battalion guns'. These had been used to varying extents after 1792, but often only for political reasons, since they were associated with the Revolutionary volunteers; they had never been popular with professional officers, least of all those of the artillery, and had been

suppressed in 1797. It is unlikely that their re-appearance just before the battle of Wagram had much effect on the enemy, although their noise and flash may have encouraged some French infantry to stand their ground. In theory two 4-pounders were supposed to be attached to each regiment, but it is unlikely that this ratio was achieved. The majority of each crew were from the infantry; in battle they man-oeuvred the guns by hand, on *bricoles*, as an integral part of their battalions.

G: SORAUREN, 28 JULY 1813: The difficulty of deployment during up-hill attacks

By early June 1813 most of the French forces had been chased out of north-western Spain; but within a month Marshal Nicolas Soult had reorganized the survivors and led them back into the Pyrenees, to re-establish contact with the garrison still holding out at Pamplona. The high water mark of this offensive came at Sorauren – only some 6 miles short of the fortress, but in an area of steep, rugged, scrub-covered terrain that made tactical movements very difficult. The illustration shows the first French attack, which was launched down a long ridge, across a deep valley, then up against a British force that was lining the next crest along the north-western side of Oricain hill. The village of Sorauren is off the bottom left of the plate, behind the French right flank.

The brigade of Gen Jean Lecamus is shown, climbing uphill in an echelon of battalion columns of divisions at half distance, the right battalion – the 31e Léger – in the lead (foreground). To its left are, successively, two battalions of the 70e de Ligne, and a single battalion of the 88e de Ligne. A strong skirmish line precedes them, totalling perhaps as many as 800 men; this is an attempt to meet the demands of the terrain, and to match the strength of the British skirmishers, who have been troublesome in previous battles. The attack is supported from a ridge to its rear (not illustrated) by the fire of four mule-packed light guns – the only type that can be moved through the mountains.

Facing this assault, BrigGen Ross has the British 20th Foot (East Devon) on his left and the 23rd Foot (Royal Welsh Fusiliers) on his right; the Portuguese 7th Cacadores and a company from the Brunswick-Oels Jägers skirmish on the forward slope, making a total of perhaps 700 in the British skirmish line. Overall, Ross is outnumbered three-to-two, and has no artillery – but he holds the vital high ground. The French have to scramble up nearly 500 feet in altitude, and during most of their climb only the British skirmishers are visible forward of the crest.

Then, as each French battalion finally approaches the crest, it is suddenly confronted by the British infantry, who loose a volley of musketry, give a bloodthirsty cheer, and immediately advance determinedly with the bayonet. After their long climb the French are unready to receive such an unexpected onslaught, and are pushed at least halfway back down the hill. The British do not pursue them far, but return to their starting positions behind the crest, to regroup and prepare for the next enemy effort. (Since the British had used these tactics in many previous Peninsular battles they can hardly be called 'novel' in 1813; indeed, they had been employed by Gen Wolfe in Canada in 1759, and a version of them had even been recommended for French use in the essays of the great Guibert.)

A Guard grenadier skirmishing in a vineyard. At Sorauren (see Plate G inset) British witnesses reported that skirmishers facing them wore bearskin bonnets. This is hardly in keeping with modern ideas of agile and inconspicuous fieldcraft; but the bearskin was a sign of élite status, and there are many references to its being carried on campaign, carefully wrapped or bagged, and put on before going into action. As described in the text, skirmishers post-1808 were certainly not limited to the voltigeur companies from each battalion. (After Raffet; Philip Haythornthwaite Collection)

General Lecamus himself was wounded in the left leg during this combat. His men renewed their attack – in a rather half-hearted manner – about two hours later. Other French brigades further east (i.e. beyond Lecamus' left flank) would all be defeated by 4pm that day, thus ending the battle of 'First Sorauren'. Fighting would resume two days later at 'Second Sorauren', when the British would attack all the way back to and beyond the original French starting position; this decisive victory spelt an end to Soult's offensive.

From the background to the foreground, we see (1) the centre and left of the French line pressing their attacks further off to the east – these met with no better success than did Lecamus. At the far right of the British position, the ruined chapel of San Salvador (2) stands on higher ground behind the military crest; anchored to this is the right half of the 23rd Foot (3). A battalion of the 88e de Ligne (4) advance against them, and one from the 70e de Ligne (5) against the left half of the 23rd; but the British battalion is concealed behind the crest, and because of the echeloning of Lecamus' units the only contact so far is between the opposing skirmish lines.

Another battalion of the 70e (6), further forward, has almost reached the crest when the right half-battalion of the 20th Foot (7) suddenly steps forward into sight and fires a volley; now they give their triumphant cheer, and are on the point of starting their counter-charge. The average strength of Lecamus' battalions is about 600 men, giving a division frontage of about 65 men; with a frontage of perhaps 150 men, the five British companies overlap them on both flanks. The French skirmishers are shot down or driven back in some confusion into their front rank, which has taken significant casualties from the volley. They do not have time to deploy from column into line, as the manual expected them to do when in close contact; they have lost momentum, and come to a stop, but they have not yet broken to the rear.

The left half-battalion of the 20th Foot (8) has just broken the column of the 31e Léger (9), which leads the echelon attack. As the redcoats charge downhill with the bayonet, very few Frenchmen – mostly officers and NCOs – stand their ground to try an unequal contest with cold steel. Actual casualties to British bayonets are few, but the French defeat is total.

The British will also be disorganized by their charge, however. Some men will break off to loot the dead and wounded, while others reload to fire into the backs of the retreating French. Their officers will have to exert all their authority to halt this freelance activity, recall their men, and re-form the line back at the top of the slope.

(Inset 1) British witnesses at Sorauren were surprised that some French skirmishers were wearing bearskins. This shows that the grenadier platoons (or in this case, the equivalent carabinier platoon of a Light Infantry regiment) were thrown forward. This was unusual, but in steep mountain terrain in the Peninsula it made perfect sense: it was impossible to conduct any but the most basic close-order manoeuvres, and then only slowly, so the élite platoons in the rear divisions would otherwise have been effectively 'left out of battle'.

(Inset 2) According to the manual there were supposed to be two or three drummers per platoon to relay simple instructions, who would live with their platoon on the march and in camp. In battle, however, they would be concentrated into a single group of 18 or 27 drums posted 15 paces behind the battalion colour party, following the third rank. If a platoon were detached, e.g. as skirmishers, they would take their drummers with them. Drummers of a Light Infantry battalion are shown here; not illustrated are the cornets (in modern terms, 'French horns') used by some Régiments d'Infantérie Légère during the Empire. These were not universally welcomed, and some officers believed that they were less audible in combat than drums.

H: WATERLOO, 18 JUNE 1815:
The attack of the Middle Guard
At perhaps 7.30–7.45pm, towards the end of a long day's fighting, the French made one final effort to break the stubborn resistance of the British-Allied army on the plateau of Mont St Jean: five battalions of the 'Middle Guard', as yet unscathed, were sent forward up the gentle slope between the farms of Hougoumont on the west and La Haie Sainte on the east. They advanced with measured step in a regulation line of battalion columns of divisions at half distance, occupying a frontage (including spaces left between units to allow for deployment) of up to 1,000 yards. Waiting at the top

they found a line of British battalions, with Nassauers on their left (eastern) flank. The latter were brushed aside by the 1er Bataillon, 3e Grenadiers à pied de la Garde Impériale; but then the decisive combat began against the British infantry – the event partly illustrated here. The average strength of the Middle Guard battalions was about 600 men.

In the foreground, opposing the attack of the 2e/3e Chasseurs, are Col Colborne's 52nd (Oxfordshire) Light Infantry, the left-hand battalion of Gen Adam's 3rd Brigade. Beyond them, Gen Maitland's Guards Brigade of two battalions (2/1st and 3/1st Foot Guards) face the advance of the 1er/3e Chasseurs and, east of them, the single battalion of the 4e Grenadiers (only the right-hand British battalion is illustrated here). East of Maitland (beyond the right edge of the illustration), the battered remnants of Gen Sir Colin Halkett's 5th Brigade – two composite British battalions, 33rd/69th and 30th/73rd – are facing the 4e Chasseurs and 1er/3e Grenadiers.

All five French battalions attempt to deploy from column into line to give fire, but only the two opposed by Maitland successfully complete the manoeuvre. This is because the 1st Foot Guards do not launch a counter-attack at close range, but stand on the spot firing volleys. This allows time for their opponents to deploy and reply in kind, at rough equality of strength, thus inevitably leading to heavy casualties on both sides (from a starting strength of about 1,080 on 18 June, Maitland's two battalions will record 492 killed and wounded). By contrast, the other three British battalions give relatively little fire, but cheer and charge in with the bayonet. As in the Peninsula, this tactic disrupts the French before they can deploy, and their columns dissolve towards the rear. This happens particularly quickly and decisively in the case of the 2e/3e Chasseurs, who are hit in the flank by the right half-battalion of the 52nd Light Infantry, echeloned by platoons.

The French retreat will be covered by two or three fresh battalions of the Old Guard waiting in the rear, but this last reserve will prove quite inadequate to stem the swelling Allied advance. As word of the Middle Guard's defeat spreads through Bonaparte's army – simultaneously threatened from the east by the Prussians – it will collapse into a general 'sauve qui peut'.

The terrain of the battlefield (1) is open farmland with standing corn, partly trampled by the cavalry charges of the afternoon but in places still affording visual cover for infantry. The 52nd Light Infantry (2) outflanks the 2e/3e Chasseurs (3) with a spirited counter-charge by the five companies of its right half-battalion. Each French division tries to form front to flank to meet the sudden threat; but although they actually manage to fire more musket shots than they receive, the entire cohesion of their battalion is destroyed, and a growing flood of fugitives makes its way to the rear. Meanwhile, the right half of Maitland's Guards Brigade (4) deliver volleys at the 1er/3e Chasseurs (5), who themselves deploy from column into line on the centre, and return volleys of their own. This firefight will continue for some time with mounting losses but no clear

result. Eventually the French battalion will give way when they realize that the units on their flanks have already retreated.

(**Inset 1**) A veteran NCO posted in from a senior battalion of Chasseurs of the Guard, in full field service uniform and bearskin, tries to exercise leadership over an ill-assorted group of raw drafts, in the motley uniforms typical of these junior battalions scraped together in a matter of weeks. The French system relied heavily upon strong 'surveillance' by older and more experienced soldiers over new arrivals.

(**Inset 2**) In any French unit's corps of drums the drum major cut a redoubtable figure. His official duty was to ensure that orders he received from senior officers were broadcast quickly and accurately by the appropriate drum signals to the troops in line. Less officially he was something of a figurehead, mascot, or even clown, as he swaggered up and down in his dazzling uniform (paid for by the regimental officers), keeping time with elaborate flourishes of his ornamental mace. No corps of drums was more splendid than that of the Foot Grenadiers of the Imperial Guard, though they are seen here in service dress – their parade uniforms were grander still.

In this free but spirited study, Raffet conveys the idea of the drum major as a sort of human flag on the battlefield: while the drums beat under his control, the battalion is still a living force. (Anne S.K.Brown Library,Providence, RI)

INDEX

Figures in **bold** refer to illustrations.

American War of Independence
(1775–1783)influence on military
thinking 5
Ancien Régime 15, 16, 25
military thinking of 3, 4, 12, 13–14
armies of Europe: manpower figures 49
artillery 4, 21, 42, 43, 45, 49, 52–53
vulnerabilities to 7
Auerstadt, battle of **E** (37, 58–60), 42
Austerlitz, battle of 41, **41**, 50, 53
Austrian troops 11–12, 27, 41

Bergen, battle of **D** (36, 57–58)
Bisson, Gen Baptiste Pierre 43
Boulogne camp of the Grande Armée 29–32
Bourcet, Pierre 4
British forces 45, 46–48
Broglie, Marshal Duke of 8, 12
Bugeaud, Marshal Thomas Robert 46
Bussaco 45, **45**

canister shot
vulnerabilities to **6**, 7
cartoons **9**
Castalla, battle of 47, **47**
cavalry 21–22, 27, 43, 45
chronology 11
Clausewitz, Karl von 31
command and communication
Drum Majors **30**, **46**, **63**
drummers **5**, **30**, 44, **44**, **46**, **56**
mounted adjutant 32, **32**
conscription and conscripts 9, 15, 17, 49
Coudray, Chevalier Tronçon du 7
Craonne, battle at 3

Davout, Marshal Louis-Nicolas 31, 41
D'Erlon, Marshal Jean-Baptiste 50
Desaix, Gen Louis Charles 28
Diersheim, battle of 17, **17**
Duhesme, Gen Count Philippe-Guillaume
17, **17**, 18–19, 31
Dumouriez, Gen Charles 11, 12, 55
Dupont, Gen Pierre 32, 43

Egypt 27, 28, **C** (35, 57)
engineers 43, 44, **44**
Essai général de tactique (Guibert) 9
Essai historique sur l'infanterie légère
(Duhesme) 19
Eylau, battle of 42

Flers, Gen 17
Fleurus, battle of 17
Folard, Jean-Charles de 7
Foy, Gen Maximillen-Sébastien 43
monument to **31**
Frederick II, 'the Great,' King of Prussia 25
French-Indian War in America 4–5
Friedland, battle of 23, 42–43

glossary 2
Grande Armée 3, 28–32, 41–43
1808 Reforms 50–53
battalion strength in 1814: 51
and battlefield overcrowding 50
Boulogne camp 29–32
campaigns of 1805–1807: 32–43
Polish campaign 42–43
quality after 1812: 49
grapeshot
vulnerabilities to **6**, 7
Gribeauval, Baptiste Vaquette de 4
Guibert, Gen Count Jacques-Antoine-
Hippolyte de (1743–1790) 7, 9, 11,
14, 17, 46–47

Hondeschoote, battle of 18

Imperial Guardsmen
in line formation **6**, **52**, **53**
and loading drill **51**, **59**
training 52
infantry tactical formations
Army Corps 22
column-line deployments **7**, **11**, 20, **20**, 42
in attack **23**, 23–26, **24**, **25**
in defence 26–27
columns 4, **4**, 5–8, 11, 14, **14**, 16, **16**,
22, **22**, 46, 49
battalions 7, **7**, 10, 29, 50
Division 22
echelons 24, 25, 28
flexibility of 41–43
lines 5–8, 10, **12**, 16, **16**
advances 4, **4**
battalions 15, **15**
'passage of lines' 10, 13, **13**
ordre mixte (composite order) 21, **21**,
22–23, 28, 43, 50
square formations 10, 22, 26, **26**, 27, **27**
infantry units 4

Jemappes, battle of 11, **A** (33, 55)
Jena, battle of 23, 41, 42
Jomini, Chef de bataillon Antoine-Henri 31,
49

Lynn, Prof John 15

Macdonald, Marshal Jacques-Etienne-Joseph-
Alexandre 23, 50, **50**
Maizeroy, Joly de 7
Manuel d'Infanterie 51
Marchand, Gen 43
Marmont, Marshal Auguste-Frédéric-Louis
23, 49, **49**
Ménil-Durand, François-Jean de 7
military theory, manuals of 31, 51
Monnier, Gen 28
Montalembert, Marc-René 4
Moore, Gen Sir John 45
Morand, Gen Charles Antoine 42, 49

Napoleon Bonaparte (1769–1821) 4, 13,
16, 21, 22, 27, 28, 32, **52**
and 'corrupt gigantism' 49–54
reorganization of State and Army 29–32
Neerwinden, battle of 12
Ney, Marshal Michel 23, 25, 29, **29**, 31, 43

Peninsular War 43–48
victories against Spain 44–46
Perpignan, battle at 17
Perulle, attack at 14, **14**
Pirmasens, battle of 24
platoon line firing 12, **12**
Polish troops 8, **8**
Prussian troops **9**, 24
Puysegur, Louis-Pierre de 7, 8
Pyramids, battle of the **C** (35, 57)

*Règlement concernant l'exercice et les
manoeuvres de l'infanterie see also*
military theory, manuals of
1791 specifications 9, 10, **10**, 12, 13, 14,
15, 22, 53
1808 revision 15, **15**, 26, 27, 31
1830s revision 54
modern ceremonial equivalent drill
practice **60**
Revolutionary France
inexperience of new troops 15, 17
offensive requirements 17
professionalism of Generals 15–16
revised military ethos of 13–20
Rottenburg, Francis de 19
roundshot
vulnerabilities to **6**
Russian troops 41, 42, 43

Saint-Cyr, Marshal Marquis Laurent Gouvion
31–32
Saragossa siege 44
Sénarmont, Gen Alexandre-Antoine de 43
Seven Years' War (1756–1763): influence
on military thinking 3–8
siege operations 44
skirmishing tactics 5, 10, 12, **12**, 13, 14, **14**,
18, 18–20, **19**, **20**, 41, 42, **62**
grandes bandes **19**, 19–20, 42
Sorauren, battle of **G** (39, 61–62), 48
Soult, Marshal Nicolas 31, 41
Spanish forces 43–46
street and house to house fighting 25, **25**, 44
Suchet 23, 47

Thionville, battle of 16, **16**

Valmy, cannonade of 11

Wagram, battle of 23, **F** (38, 60–61), 50, 53
Waterloo, battle of **H** (40, 62–63), 50, 53
Wattignies, battle of 11, **B** (34, 55–57)

Young Guards 3, **3**